ART THERAPY
WITH SEXUAL ABUSE SURVIVORS

ABOUT THE AUTHOR

Stephanie L. Brooke, MS, NCC worked as a social worker at Hillside Children's Center, working with emotionally disturbed and aggressive adolescents in an independent living facility. Many of the clients had sexual abuse survivor issues. She received training as an art therapist at Hillside Children's Center in Rochester, New York. Ms. Brooke conducts individual, family, and group counseling with an emphasis on art therapy as a therapeutic approach. Specifically, she specializes in sexual abuse issues. Additionally, Ms. Brooke is an instructor at Geneseo Community College in Lakeville, New York, teaching psychology, sociology, child development, and human relations. For the past sixteen years, she has been a dedicated pastel artist.

ART THERAPY WITH SEXUAL ABUSE SURVIVORS

By

STEPHANIE L. BROOKE, MS, NCC

With a Foreword by

Dee Spring, PhD, A.T.R. - BC, BFCE

CHARLES C THOMAS · PUBLISHER, LTD.
Springfield · Illinois · U.S.A.

Published and Distributed Throughout the World by
CHARLES C THOMAS · PUBLISHER, LTD.
2600 South First Street
Springfield, Illinois 62794-9265

© *1997 by* CHARLES C THOMAS · PUBLISHER, LTD.
ISBN 0-398-06805-4 (cloth)
ISBN 0-398-06806-2 (paper)
Library of Congress Catalog Card Number: 97–22272

Printed in the United States of America
OL-R-3

Library of Congress Cataloging-in-Publication Data

Brooke, Stephanie L.
    Art therapy with sexual abuse survivors / by Stephanie L.
Brooke: with a foreword by Dee Spring.
      p.   cm.
    Includes bibliographical references and index.
    ISBN 0–398–06805–4 (cloth) – ISBN 0–398–06806–2 (pbk.)
    1. Adult child sexual abuse victims – Rehabilitation. 2. Art
therapy. I. Title.
RC569.5.A28B77 1997
616.85 ' 8369065156 – dc21

                                        97–22272
                                          CIP

FOREWORD

Art expression articulates the layered communication about forgotten or remembered events. Past experience, associated feelings, and references cannot be eliminated from artwork created in the present. Impressions build one upon the other and are influenced by their predecessor. Art reflects and incorporates past experience, its impact on current emotional reaction, and subsequent behavior. The feelings bonded to those events serve as reflectors through form as content. The communication of image in art expression is a silent, visual language, translated into linguistic form through retrocognition, examination, and experiencing the art object. Art making functions as a sender, the image as a message, the art maker as a receiver. Images in art expression, like dreams, are rooted in the personal history, incorporate current events, and in some form, express a wish for the future.

I call this the *image triad.* Images may remain internal, or be projected onto a tangible surface in the form of artistic expression. Since images are reflections of a field of view, they provide a schema or likeness that is within the constructs of the individual. As images build one upon the other, they arouse associations. The use of art expression in a directed and sequential manner prompts the emergence of historic information that has been stored in various caches of the mind.

Hidden images and responses to traumatic events tend to surface in a safe environment. The images originate during the traumatic experience, then stored in what we call the "unconscious" until the patient has decided that the original threat is no longer valid. First, the victim-artist must learn what has happened in the past. Next, the experience must be revisited in all its aspects: mental images, physical response (body memory), associated emotions, and references. Then, the historic experience must be reflected upon in a cognitive manner and processed from the adult point of view to form a new perspective. The final step involves the resolution of personal truth, the acceptance that the past cannot be changed, and that there is a grieving for what is perceived as lost. These steps lead to trauma synthesis and to the time when it no longer hurts to remember.

During the process of trauma synthesis, distortion (visual or verbal) may occur. The content of the remembrance is represented by symbolic form which prompts other associations, references, metaphors, or parables. As more information is gained, details of historic experience may seem to change from the original story. Information may become more detailed as dissociated material is retrieved and processed. Regardless of the method of presentation, the reported scenes represent individual stories, including distortions, similar to the way history came down through the generations before there was written word. Pictorial form seems to be the most efficient and succinct method to communicate complex issues. Particular feelings may be attached to the images (dissociated materials in symbolic form). The reactions to the image are symptoms which emerge from dissociated material, commonly referred to as posttraumatic stress. It is important to identify the feeling and its connection to the image, as the image is the message.

During the course of therapy, the visual dialogue captures the missing pieces (image as messages) that are attached to art products created by victim-artists. Over time, the images go together in a composite (visual dialogue) that articulates past experience through recurring images, connecting history to current events. My empirical, quantitative research (1975-1988) on sexual abuse, posttraumatic stress, and artistic symbolic language concluded that there are two primary, consistent forms incorporated in the artistic symbolic language used by victims of sexual trauma. These consistent forms are wedges (threat) and disembodied/highly stylized eyes (guilt). These forms are the beginning of an alphabet that concretely differentiates traumatic and dissociative disorders from other disorders and experiences. This artistic language is also consistently created by individuals diagnosed with Dissociative Identity Disorder. Other population do not *consistently* use these forms in their art products. In this book, Stephanie Brooke refers to the emergence of this artistic language, and her own viewing of victim-artists' art products which reveal symbolic forms.

Art Therapy With Sexual Abuse Survivors seeks to examine the most basic art therapy approaches to treatment of traumatic conditions due to sexual exploitation or abuse. The book is not structured around new or specialized ideas for treatment. Rather, the focus is a commentary on a collection of publications of art therapists and others who have written on the subject. The book includes a general reporting of material to various art therapy approaches and orientations. The theme throughout the book is on the importance of capturing iconographic material, through the use of art therapy., to assess and/or treat individuals who have experienced sexual abuse. I believe the collective content of the book to be especially important to art therapists who are just beginning to work with this victim population. The book provides a compendium and review of a number of historical and controversial areas that are important to art therapists and other disciplines.

Dee Spring, PhD, A.T.R.-BC, MFCC
Executive Director
Earthwood Center
Ventura, California

PREFACE

S exual abuse survivor issues began coming to the forefront in the 1980s when I was earning my B.A. in Clinical Counseling Psychology. Survivors from all walks of life were coming forward to tell their story. Additionally, therapists began to focus more on these issues when working with their clients. One mode of therapy that was promising in promoting healing and growth was art therapy.

The purpose of this book is to provide therapists, who use art as an adjunct therapy or primary therapy, with an overview of art therapy with sexual abuse survivors. This text may be particularly helpful for the beginning art therapist who has little experience with sexual abuse issues. The book discusses art therapy assessment, graphic indicators of abuse, traumatic memory, and legal issues. Additionally, it will focus on research and case illustrations of individual, family, and group art therapy.

Chapter 1 presents an introduction on the use of art therapy with sexual abuse survivors, including various definitions of sexual abuse. Chapter 2 focuses on art therapy assessments including strengths and weaknesses. Graphic indicators of sexual abuse are discussed in Chapter 3. Chapter 4 debates the use of art therapy in with memories of sexual abuse. Chapter 5 reports on the legal issues of using drawings in court proceedings and the ability of art therapists to serve as expert witnesses. Chapters 6 through 11 present case illustrations of individual, group, and family art therapy. Finally, Chapter 12 provides a brief summary of the book.

ACKNOWLEDGMENTS

There are many individuals that I would like to express my appreciation to in the completion of this work. First, I am grateful to the art therapists who contributed to this book, including Ellen Horovitz, M.A., ATR; Felice Cohen, M.S., ATR; and Dee Spring, PhD, ATR-BC, BFCE. In addition, I am grateful to Maria Worth, CSW, ACSW, who co-led the family therapy sessions. I would like to thank Else Capell, MST, ATR-BC, who supervised my initial art therapy hours at Hillside. Also, I appreciate assistance with the artwork for this book that was provided by Mike and Georgia Girhard.

CONTENTS

ART THERAPY
WITH SEXUAL ABUSE SURVIVORS

Chapter 1

INTRODUCTION

S exual abuse is a recurring problem in our culture resulting in a myriad of treatment issues for survivors. Although there are a variety of therapeutic approaches for working with this population, art therapy is one which may be less threatening since it does not rely heavily on a verbal mode of communication. The purpose of this book is to focus on treatment approaches, including individual, group, and family art therapy. Case examples with illustrations are presented. Additionally, the book discusses graphic indicators of sexual abuse, along with the issue of forgotten memories and the false memory debate. Also, legal matters of using art therapy assessments in the court system and art therapists serving as expert witnesses will be addressed. This chapter provides a brief introduction to art therapy and the dynamics of different art products. Various definitions of sexual abuse are presented.

DEVELOPMENT OF ART THERAPY

Normal persons, children, who are involved in either personal or situational stress (such as sexual abuse) are temporarily vulnerable to developing emotional problems. The arts must be made available to these children to facilitate coping skills in the face of life-threatening trauma. (White House Commission on Mental Health, 1978; cited in Sgroi, 1982)

Throughout our history, art has served as a visual record of cultural, social and political issues of that time. On a personal level, art conveys the emotions, thoughts, feelings as well as the conflicts of the artist. Since art expression does not rely on verbal expression, therapists began using art as a diagnostic tool when working with clients. In the 1930s, art therapy emerged as a treatment modality.

Due to the increasing isolation, dehumanization, and over intellectualization of our culture, there is an increasing focus on affect and getting in touch with the inner self (Moreno, 1975). Accordingly, therapists are inclined to use nonverbal approaches such as art, music, dance, and drama for psychological healing and growth. Although these methods may be unorthodox to some, people have the opportunity to access information that eludes their perception by approaching problem solving through the modality of art therapy.

Art has been used as a means of self-expression for centuries. People have used art materials to "make images and connect them to feelings and bodily states [that] bring into the open thoughts that have been only vaguely sensed" (Keyes, 1983, p. 104). Edwards (1986) noted that drawing exists as a parallel to verbal language and is the simplest of all nonverbal languages. Art does not have the restriction of linguistic development in order to convey thoughts or feelings.

> Aside from the therapeutic benefit of nonverbal communication of thoughts and feelings, one of the most impressive aspects of the art process is its potential to achieve or restore psychological equilibrium. This use of the art process as intervention is not mysterious or particularly novel; it may have been one of the reasons humankind developed art in the first place-to alleviate or contain feelings of trauma, fear, anxiety, and psychological threats to the self and the community. (Malchiodi, 1990, p. 5)

Projective methods designed to explore motivation are not new to the field of psychotherapy. Machover (1949) observed the power of projective methods in discovering unconscious determinants of self-expression that are not apparent in direct, verbal communication. Langer (1957) stressed that "there is an important part of reality that is quite inaccessible to the formative influence of language: that is the realm of the so called "inner experience," the life of feeling and emotion, the primary function of art is to objectify feelings so that we can contemplate and understand it" (p. 4-5). Naumburg (1966), a renowned art therapist, asserted that "by projecting interior images into exteriorized designs art therapy crystallizes and fixes in lasting form the recollections of dreams of phantasies which would otherwise remain evanescent and might quickly be forgotten" (p. 2).

Due to the increasing number of therapists who utilized art as a method of therapy, the American Art Therapy Association (AATA) was created in 1969 to set standards for certification and registration of art therapists. Art therapy was described as follows (cited in Levick, 1983, p. 3-4):

> Art therapy provides the opportunity for nonverbal expression and communication. The use of art as therapy implies that the creative process can be a means of both reconciling emotional conflicts and of fostering self-awareness and personal growth. When using art as a vehicle for psychotherapy, both product and the associative references may be used in an effort to help the individual find a more compatible relationship between his inner and outer worlds.

Naumburg (1966) was one of the first individuals to utilize art therapy when working with her clients. It was her opinion that visual projections and unconscious material were frequently expressed more directly in pictures. In discussing art therapy, she made the following point:

> Pictured projections of unconscious material escape censorship more easily than do verbal expressions, so that the therapeutic process is speeded up...the productions are durable and unchanging; the content cannot be erased by forgetting, and their authorship is hard to deny. (Naumburg, 1966, p. 512)

Ulman was another forerunner in the field of art therapy. Although Naumburg began her work as a psychologist, Ulman was an art teacher at the time she began her career in the field of art therapy. As Naumburg, Ulman adopted the psychodynamic perspective. In discussing art therapy, Ulman stated that the motivation to produce art derives from the personality as an attempt to bring order out of chaos (Ulman & Dachinger 1975). Additionally, Ulman felt that the art process allowed the person to learn about herself and the world and establish a relation between the two. "In the complete creative process, inner and outer realities are fused into a new identity" (cited in Rubin, 1987, p. 281).

Also having a psychodynamic orientation was Kramer (1971) who came to the field after Naumburg. Whereas Naumburg was known for her analytically-oriented approach to art therapy, Kramer was noted for her emphasis on the significance of art (Harris & Joseph, 1973). According to Kramer (1971), "art is characterized by economy of means, inner consistency, and evocative power" (p. 50). Kramer was interested in examining the psychological processes that are active when art is made. She described art as follows:

> ...a means of widening the range of human experiences by creating equivalents for such experiences... Using these equivalents the artist can choose,

vary, and repeat what experiences he will. He can reexperience, resolve, and integrate conflict. (Kramer, 1979, p. 8)

Stember (1977) was an art therapist whose contributions led to the development of Connecticut's Sexual Trauma Treatment Program for sexually abused children. She combined several theoretical perspectives when using art therapy with sexually abused children. Stember stressed that first drawings are vitally important:

> The first drawings relate intimately to the impulses, anxieties, conflicts and compensations that are characteristic of that individual. In some sense, these drawings are the person at that moment. [Therefore] we can analyze some of the work, process behavior and product in terms of where symbols, forms, were placed on the sheet [of paper] and the [rapidity and repetitiousness] of graphic movement (whether they start small and tight and move outward or start large, scrawling, chaotic and diffused) and in recognition of diffusion and chaos-attempt to integrate the forms into a unified whole. (Stember, 1977; cited in Sgroi, 1982)

For a child, expression through art may be a nonthreatening means of expressing feelings and fears. Kramer (1971) discovered that art therapy helps a child master anxiety and make emotional preparations for change or transition. Through art, a child can fulfill wishes or express emotions which he/she may not be able to do in reality. Additionally, the child can learn to control the real world by experimenting with art and the thoughts and feelings illustrated in the creative process (Rubin, 1984). Researchers have found that the tactile and symbolic nature of art therapy allows the client to bring overwhelming and powerful emotions into consciousness thereby, permitting the client to master and integrate these emotions (Robbins & Seaver, 1976; Myers-Garrett, 1987).

APPROACHES TO ART EXPRESSION

Although art therapy derived from a Freudian perspective, a variety of theoretical approaches have emerged. The following theories will be described briefly: Psychoanalytic, Jungian, Gestalt, Developmental, Cognitive, and Group. These represent only a few of the theoretical approaches to art therapy. Research presented in this book utilizes these styles of therapy. Rather than adhering to one theoretical perspective, many of the therapists incorporate aspects of a variety of theoretical approaches in their treatment plans.

The forerunners of art therapy, Naumburg, Ulman, and Kramer, had a psychoanalytic orientation. This approach emphasized the importance of dreams in understanding the unconscious determinants of behavior (Corsini & Wedding, 1989). Art therapists working from this orientation will examine spontaneous drawings including those involving dreams and wishes (Rubin, 1987). As with free association, dream interpretation is unstructured and provides the artist with the freedom of expression that is not limited by language skills. Issues of transference are often worked through in order to uncover distorted perceptions based on unresolved conflicts from the past (Rubin, 1987). Decoding symbolic meanings associated with images is sometimes interpreted rigidly with this approach. Aware of this limitation, Naumburg (1966) stated that the only valid interpretation of an image comes from the artist.

Supporting the view that behavior is based on unconscious forces, the Jungian orientation interprets dreams as messages from the unconscious mind (Corsini & Wedding, 1989). Jung, a novice artist, worked through his own conflicts by painting and sculpting: "In fact, Jung's theories can best be understood in the context of the value he attached to the subjective reality of spontaneously generated images" (Rubin, 1987, p. 93). One aspect of Jung's theory of personality centered on archetypes which he described as latent thought-forms inherited by individuals: "Such images are not based on our personal life experiences, although they are activated by them; they are found universally" (DiCaprio, 1983, p. 88). A dialogue with the unconscious is stimulated by having the artist personify images or archetypes (Rubin, 1987). Elements, such as the shadow (dark side of person) are brought to light by personifying the image. Revelation of these aspects of the self will help the person work towards an integrated whole. Rubin (1987) stressed that some archetypical images, "being collective rather than personal, can never be fully assimilated, and it would be more accurate to describe the therapeutic goal as learning to trust the inner figures, as sources of insight and creative development in the individuation process" (p. 105).

As opposed to psychoanalytic therapy, Gestalt art therapy, began by Dr. Janie Rhyne, is nondirective. Gestalt therapists will not focus on interpretation, rather they will assist the client in expanding his/her awareness through active experiencing of the art image (Rhyne, 1973). One means of increasing awareness is by concentrating on dreams. When working with dream images, a therapist using a Gestalt approach will ask the client to enact a figure in a dream: "Clients can best process their dreams by "becoming" the objects in them and thus reown "disowned parts" (Rubin, 1987, p. 304). This is similar to the Jungian theory of personification. The Gestalt method is primarily affective, focusing on feelings and the recognition of one's feelings (Rhyne, 1973; Corsini & Wedding, 1989).

> The reason drawing or painting may be "therapeutic" is that, when experienced as a process, it allows the artist to know himself as a whole person within a relatively short period of time. He not only becomes aware of internal movement toward experiential wholeness, but he also receives visual confirmation of such movement from the drawings he produces. (Zinker, 1977, p. 236)

Expression through art helps the person experience the inner self and integrate aspects of the self that may have been formerly denied (Rubin, 1987).

Developmental art therapy is especially useful for assessing age appropriate performance. Erikson's (1950) theory of development in addition to Lowenfeld and Brittain's (1987) stages of artistic proficiency is helpful. Using the developmental approach, a therapist will try to determine those issues affecting the client. Whether working with children or adults, an understanding of the client's developmental level, psychologically as well as artistically, is essential for guiding the course of treatment. The developmental approach begins with a nondirective segment in which the therapist offers a wide selection of materials and allows the artist to determine the theme, activity, and content. The next phase is directive, in which the therapist structures particular activities for the purpose of determining the client's level of skill, organization in the use of materials, response to media properties, and ability to express affect (Rubin, 1987).

The cognitive approach to art therapy explores emotions and thoughts. The main premise is to ease tensions and to build self-confidence. This method is particularly useful for individuals who experience difficulty in articulating thoughts and feelings in words (Rubin, 1987). For these clients, the metaphor of "right brain" thinking may be preferred; therefore, they need a channel of communication that can bypass the verbal mode. Free drawings are particularly useful for determining cognition. One art therapy assessment, the Silver Drawing Test (SDT), measures a person's cognitive skills and adjustment. According to Silver (1990), the SDT has four goals: (1) to bypass language in assessing the ability to solve conceptual problems; (2) to provide precision in evaluating cognitive strengths or weaknesses that may not be detected by verbal measures; (3) to facilitate identification of children or adolescents who may be depressed; and (4) to provide a pre-post instrument for assessing the effectiveness of therapeutic or educational programs. By detecting low levels of cognitive development, the SDT may recognize individuals in need of new educational programs and/or counseling. Silver (1990) designed the SDT based on the theory that drawings can be used to identify and evaluate problem-solving capabilities.

Group therapy postulates that people learn and develop in the context of relationships with others. Much of the material to date with survivors of sexual abuse utilizes a group format. The rational for group work is that it provides a sense of universality with others who have shared similar experiences. As a result, the group format allows for immediate feedback and revelation of relationship patterns. Additionally, some of the goals for group counseling are the development of trust in one's self and others, increasing self-confidence, and achieving self-knowledge. These goals appear to be particularly relevant when working with survivors.

This discussion centered on a few art therapy perspectives. Several perspectives were not discussed such as existential, object relations, behavioral, humanistic, and hypnoanalytic. It is beyond the scope of this text to present information on all the art therapy theoretical perspectives. Rather, it was intended to provide a brief discussion of some perspectives that were used in research with survivors of sexual abuse. The next section will focus on a few types of art media and their clinical significance.

DYNAMICS OF ART EXPRESSION

Art therapy offers a variety of media for the client to express loss or release stress. Paint, pastels, ink, clay, and wood are some of the materials that clients can manipulate when creating art. Texture of the material is often a reflection of the artist's inner experience:

> Paint by its very nature, can elicit affective material; in combination with a
> rather kinesthetic activity (the making of lines across a large paper), it can
> become very aggressive. (Malchiodi, 1990, p. 21)

The texture of art materials can be used to reflect, mirror, or
compliment psychological states of mind (Robbins, 1987). Rubin
(1984) felt that the more unstructured the medium, the more the
client will be able to project upon it. She tends to work from simple
media and progresses to more complex ones.

Watercolors involve complex layering. This medium is
unpredictable and transparent in nature which allows the artist
spontaneous expression. Since watercolors are hard to control,
Robbins (1987) asserted that people who employ this medium are
spontaneous individuals who accept change and relinquish
omnipotence. Working with oils is a time-consuming process because
it entails layering. People who use this medium are described as
patient, allow change, and prefer a predetermined challenge
(Robbins, 1987). The use of pencil suggests a need for control,
structure, and firm boundaries (Robbins, 1987). Finger paint is a
direct form of expression. Betensky (1973) described finger paint as
an agent of regression which serves an important outlet for stress.
The use of clay involves more movement and manipulation. Clay has
served as an outlet for contained emotions such as aggression and
anger: "...those dealing with contained rage associated with early
self-object relations can benefit from large muscle activities and more
aggressive use of materials" (Robbins, 1987, p. 113). The characteristics of art materials have been utilized by art therapists for diagnostic
purposes:

> As one avenue to self-definition, we have usually had some choice of art
> materials, and have on occasion asked that people define themselves by
> choosing to be an art medium or process, and sharing their reasons. We
> have found that their choice is intimately related to how they see them-
> selves, i.e. soft or hard, flexible or firm, fragile or strong, colorful or bland,
> etc. The choice of medium then evolves into a productive activity with that
> medium, in both cases self-defining and enhancing self-awareness.
> (Moreno, 1975, p. 113)

In addition to freedom to choose art material, art therapists may
also allow freedom to choose what to draw or what to create.
Spontaneous drawings are particularly revealing for child clients.
This nondirective approach often enhances the ego of the child:
"Choice is particularly important for children from violent homes

because these children may feel that their present life experiences offer little choice and control" (Malchiodi, 1990, p. 101).

When examining a painting, art therapists will focus on the following dimensions: medium, organization, use of space and balance, form, color, line, focus or direction, motion, detail, content, affect, and effort of investment (Wadeson, 1987). Sculptures on the other hand are examined for size, mass, negative space, soundness of structure, texture, attention to detail, content, affect, and effort investment (Wadeson, 1987). For example, representations which are overly concrete suggest a rigid or narrow view of reality, a rigid defense system, and ego structure (Robbins, 1987).

Kramer (1979) observed that the ability to use lines in creating symbols develops prior to the manipulation of clay and paint. Lines are a rich form of expression that have " a life of their own, that they can be quite emotional or rational in a variety of ways, and that they can relate to their lines on the same paper" (Betensky, 1973). Lines express movement and mood.

Color may serve as a visual statement of the artist's state of mind (Robbins, 1987). Generally, yellow and orange are associated with pleasant emotions whereas violet is associated with unpleasant emotions (Ulman & Levy, 1980). The following represents affective associations to color (Alschuler & Hattwick, 1947; Klepsch & Logie, 1982):

Red - violence, excessive emotion, reflection of acute emotional experience that may be hostile or affectionate in nature

Yellow - hostility, dependency, infantile behavior

Orange - discomfort, good relationship with environment, fearful of emotional expression

Blue - controlled reactions, self-restraint, conforming

Green - controlled behavior, least driven by emotion

Brown - timidity, regression, reflect desire to smear

Black - controlled reactions, intellectual, compulsive, depression, emotional repression, anxiety

Art therapists have usually associated black with states of depression or anxiety (Klepsch & Logie, 1982; Malchiodi, 1990). The use of red, particularly on doors or entries into a home, is used by some sexual abuse survivors (Malchiodi, 1990).

> If, in fact, patients choose colors that express their current emotional states, we as therapists can suggest other colors to create a dialogue incontrasts and alternatives... the therapist attempts to integrate polarities and splits within the psychic organization that are expressed through color and that ultimately parallel and metaphorically describe the affective states of the patient's internal representations. (Robbins, 1987, p. 108)

Art therapists will also examine overt and covert content of an art product in addition to the behaviors and verbalizations that occur while the artist is working. Rubin (1984) emphasized that it is important to observe the artist's behavior before and after the product is complete. How the artist uses the materials is also enlightening. For instance, chaotic discharge will involve spilling, splashing, pounding, and destruction of materials (Kramer, 1971).

As with other forms of psychotherapy, art therapy occasionally evokes resistance. This resistance may take a variety of forms such as an unwillingness to create, the use of impersonal imagery, turning to (cartoon) humor, a regression to earlier forms of art behavior, and a compulsive fussing over details (Rubin, 1984). Kramer (1971) noted that defense occurs in the stereotypical handling of materials, such as using only one color. In addition, defense arises through the depiction of stereotypic or repetitive forms (Malchiodi, 1990). When resistance breaks down, the art therapist can begin to interpret the meaning of the art product. One major concern is the system of interpretation. Singular and/or concrete interpretations of any aspect of art expression can lead to highly dubious conclusions.

SEXUAL ABUSE DEFINED

Although legal definitions vary from state to state, Kosof (1985) defined sexual abuse as any sexual relationship between a child and an adult (with parental authority) or any sexual act between siblings. Additionally, Kosof stated that:

> The child, harboring anger, guilt, and a frightening secret, experiences immense confusion...[it] defies the belief that the parent is the source of

trust, security, and guidance. It confuses the notion of affection and love. It alienates the child from the mother and father. It accelerates the child's sexual development and destroys the normal process of sexual maturation and growth. (Kosof, 1985, p. 63)

Maltz and Holman (1987) support Kosof's definition of sexual abuse. Further, they point out that sexual abuse includes sexual activity that occurs only once as well as that which takes place over a period of years. The term, sexual abuse, is used throughout this text and incorporates incestuous activity. Although incest is a form of sexual abuse, it is important to note the difference in these terms:

> Incest and sexual abuse are sometimes confused, but they are not the same. Sexual abuse normally refers to sexual relations between an adult and a child. Incest refers to sexual relationship between two family members whose marriage would be proscribed by law or custom... For our purposes, we will use incest to mean sexual contact between family members, including not just intercourse but also mutual masturbation, hand-genital or oral-genital contact, sexual fondling, exhibition, and even sexual proposi-tioning. (Finkelhor, 1979, p. 83-84)

According to Gil (1983), sexual abuse transpires when a person, adult or child, forces, tricks, threatens, or coerces an individual to have any kind of sexual contact with him/her. Gil (1983) asserted that "showing children pornographic pictures or films, or telling them explicitly sexual stories can be a form of sexual abuse" (Gil, 1983, p. 16). Although cultures may differ in descriptions of this taboo, sexual abuse can be roughly defined as "the engaging of a child in sexual activities that the child does not understand, to which the child cannot give informed consent, or which violate the social taboos of society" (Krugman, 1986, p. 26).

I teach psychology, sociology, child development and human relations at Genesee Community College in Lakeville, New York. As part of my lecture on sexual abuse, I present the following informa-tion to my students:

SEXUALLY ABUSIVE BEHAVIORS

- Adult or sibling sexually touching child (i.e. fondling, sexual hugs, rubbing, bathing with child, inappropriate cleaning, pinching)
- Having child touch adult/sibling sexually
- Photographing child for sexual purposes (this does not include

    photographing children naked or bathing for documentary purposes)
- Sexualized talk (i.e., suggestive language, flirtations, propositioning, romanticized language)
- Showing child pornographic materials or making them available to the child often done under the guise of educating child; to encourage child to copy sexual behaviors
- Making fun of or ridiculing the child's sexual development, preferences, or organs (i.e., comparing one child's penis to another child's or adult's penis)
- Adult exposing his/her genitals to the child for sexual gratification (i.e., strip tease, help with dressing, showing nude photos of self, inappropriate dress)
- Masturbating or otherwise being sexual in front of children (intentional exhibitionism; often under the guise of sex education)
- Voyeurism (watching someone change, peepholes, watching teenagers make out; walking into the bathroom without permission)
- Forcing overly rigid rules on dress or overly revealing dress
- Stripping to hit or spank, or getting sexual excitement out of hitting
- Verbal and emotional abuse of a sexual nature (i.e., "mother fucker", "faggot," "prick," "cock sucker")
- Having the child be sexual with animals
- Engaging the child in prostitution (observing; soliciting; or participating)
- Witnessing others being sexually abused

These are just a few definitions of sexual abuse. For the purposes of this book, sexual abuse is defined as an abuse of power: Using sex as the method in which power is taken by abusing one's position of power to influence, coerce, or otherwise engage a child or adolescent into a sexual relationship that is considered taboo by one's society. The next chapter will briefly discuss a few of the art therapy assessments that are used when evaluating cases of sexual abuse.

REFERENCES

Alschuler, R.H., & Hattwick, L.B.: *Painting and personality.* Chicago University of Chicago Press, 1947.

Betensky, M.: *Self-discovery through self-expression: Use of art in psychotherapy,* Springfield, IL: Charles C Thomas, 1973.

Corsini, R. J. & Wedding, D.: *Current psychotherapies.* Itasca, IL, F.E. Peacock, Inc, 1989.

DiCaprio, N.S.: *Personality theories: A guide to human nature.* New York, CBS College Publishing, 1983.

Edwards, B.: *Drawing on the artist within.* New York, Simon & Schuster, 1986.

Erikson, E.: *Childhood and society.* New York, Norton, 1950.

Finkelhor, D.: *Sexually victimized children.* New York, Free Press, 1979.

Gil, E.: *Outgrowing the pain.* Walnut Creek, California, Launch Press, 1983.

Harris, J. & Joseph, C.: *Murals of the mind: Image of a psychiatric community.* New York: International Universities Press, 1973.

Keyes, M.F.: *Inward journey: Art as therapy.* Lasalle, IL, Open Court, 1983.

Klepsch, M., & Logie, L.: *Children draw and tell: An introduction to the projective uses of children's human figure drawings.* New York, Brunner/Mazel, 1982.

Kosof, A.: *Incest: Families in crisis.* New York, Franklin Watts, 1985.

Kramer, E.: *Art as therapy with children.* New York, Schocken Books, 1971.

Kramer, E.: *Childhood and art therapy: Notes on theory and application.* New York, Schocken Books, 1979.

Krugman, R.: Recognition of sexual abuse in children. *Pediatrics in Review, 8(1):* 25-39, 1986.

Langer, S.K.: *Problems of art.* New York, Charles Schribner's Sons, 1957.

Levick, M.F.: *They could not talk so they drew.* Springfield, IL, Charles C Thomas, 1983.

Lowenfeld, V., & Brittain, W.L.: *Creative and mental growth.* (8th ed.). New York, Macmillan, 1987.

Machover, K.: *Personality projection in drawing of the human figure.* Springfield, IL, Charles C Thomas, 1949.

Malchiodi, C.A.: *Breaking the silence: Art therapy with children from violent homes.* New York, Brunner/Mazel, 1990.

Maltz, W. & Holman, B.: *Incest and sexuality.* Lexington, MA, Lexington Books, 1987.

Moreno, Z.T.: *Group psychotherapy and psychodrama.* New York, Beacon House, 1975.

Myers-Garrett, E.A.: The role of contours in symbol building with a victim of sexual abuse. *Pratt Institute Creative Arts Therapy Review, 8:* 45-51, 1987.

Naumburg, M.: *Dynamically oriented art therapy.* New York, Grune & Stratton, 1966.

Rhyne, J.: *The gestalt art experience.* Monterey, CA, Brooks/Cole, 1973.

Robbins, A.: *The artist as therapist.* New York, Human Sciences Press, 1987.

Robbins, A., & Seaver, L.S.: *Creative art therapy.* New York, Pratt Institute, 1976.

Rubin, J.A.: *Child art therapy.* New York, Van Nostrand Reinhold, 1984.

Rubin, J.A.: *Approaches to art therapy.* New York, Brunner/Mazel, 1987.

Sgroi, S.M.: *Handbook of clinical intervention in child sexual abuse.* Lexington, MA, Lexington Books, 1982.

Silver, R.: *Silver Drawing Test of Cognitive Skills and Adjustment.* Sarasota, FL, Ablin Press, 1990.

Stember, C.J.: *Use of art therapy in child abuse/neglect: Are there any graphic clues?* The Dynamics of Creativity, 8th Annual Conference of the American Art Therapy Association, 73-78, 1977.

Ulman, E., & Dachinger, P.: *Art therapy in theory and practice.* New York, Schocken Books, 1975.

Ulman, E. & Levy, C.A.: *Art therapy viewpoints.* New York, Schocken Books, 1980.

Wadeson, H.: *The dynamics of art psychotherapy.* New York, John Wiley, 1987.

Zinker, J.: *Creative process in Gestalt therapy.* New York, Brunner/Mazel, 1977.

Chapter 2

ART THERAPY ASSESSMENTS

There are several art therapy evaluations that may be used when working with sexual abuse survivors. This chapter will focus on the strengths and weaknesses of ten art therapy assessments. Recommendations will be made based on the assessment's reliability and validity evidence as well as the desirable and undesirable features. Additionally, the clinical usefulness of the test will be evaluated based upon research to date and my clinical experience. For additional information regarding reliability, validity, and research evidence, refer to *Tools of the Trade: A Therapist's Guide To Art Therapy Assessments* (Brooke, 1996).

HUMAN FIGURE DRAWING TEST (1968)

Human figure drawings have often been used when working with sexual abuse survivors. The Human Figure Drawing Test (HFD) was discussed in detail by Koppitz (1968). She conducted thorough research to provide evidence for the usefulness of the HFD. Koppitz (1968) clearly described developmental items and emotional indicators of human figure drawings by utilizing case studies. School achievement, cognitive development, organic conditions, and personality characteristics were a few of the topics Koppitz (1968) discussed. Interpretation of the HFDs was based on case studies, which has limitations. Additionally, quantitative scoring procedures were not demonstrated in the case examples.

Koppitz' (1968) HFD did provide validity evidence. The HFD was able to discriminate high achievers from low achievers. Although Koppitz found that the HFD differentiated between shy and aggressive children, other researchers were unable to produce the same results (Lingren, 1971; Norford & Barakat, 1990). Koppitz (1968) purported that the HFD could be used as a measure of intelligence, I agree with Motta et al. (1993) who argued that the HFD was not a reliable or valid instrument for assessing intelligence. Information on the reliability of the HFD needs to be examined. Since the standardization sample was selected over 30 years ago, future research should focus on reestablishing norms for the HFD. Clinicians may use the HFD in conjunction with other assessments in order to provide information on client issues.

In my work with sexual abuse survivors, omission of body parts was a common feature of HFDs. Additionally, sexual abuse survivors sometimes draw the head and neglect the lower portion of the body. This assessment does require clinical experience when interpreting drawings. It is recommended that the HFD not be used as a measure of intelligence; rather, as a tool to illuminate client concerns and self-perceptions. It may be a particularly useful tool when working with sexual abuse survivors.

DRAW A PERSON: SCREENING PROCEDURE FOR EMOTIONAL DISTURBANCE (1991)

The DAP: SPED (Naglieri et al., 1991) was developed to serve as a tool in the identification of children or adolescents who may be behaviorally or emotionally disturbed. Case examples were well structured and demonstrated the scoring system adequately. To date, this assessment had one of the largest and most clearly defined standardization samples. Instructions for administration, scoring, and interpretation were very detailed, yet clear.

Construct validity evidence was lacking. This was a general complaint about most human figure drawing tests (Motta et al., 1993). On the other hand, discriminant validity evidence was moderate to strong. The DAP: SPED appeared to differentiate between normal populations and special populations. Reliability evidence was strong. Although the manual stated that the drawings could be used as measures of intellectual functioning, there was no evidence provided. Therefore, the DAP: SPEED should not be used as a measure of intelligence. I highly recommend the DAP: SPEED, especially in cases where a child or adolescent is suspected to suffer from emotional disturbance.

KINETIC FAMILY DRAWINGS (1972)

Family drawings are particularly useful when trying to ascertain if a child has been sexually abused. They are helpful in revealing the nature of relationships between family members or significant individuals in the household. Generally, kinetic drawings tend to provide more information than static drawings. Burns and Kaufman (1972) added a kinetic component to traditional family drawings to create the Kinetic Family Drawing (KFD).

The KFD depicts a person's familial relationships and issues. Burns and Kaufman (1972) utilized case examples which yielded valuable information about familial relationships as well as self-concept. The authors created a grid to quantify information about the KFD; yet, they did not present guidelines for the interpretation of measurements.

There was very little information on how the test was developed. Additionally, no information was given on who was able to administer the KFD and their qualifications. Interpretation may be difficult given the ambiguity in the test terms and lack of examples for the grid information. Objective scoring systems have been developed for the KFD (Cummings, 1980; Mostkoff & Lazarus, 1983). With training, interrater reliability has been established (McPhee & Wegner, 1976). Test-retest reliability evidence was weak, suggesting that the KFD may be sensitive to mood changes. Validity evidence was also mixed. Studies that examined the KFD as a possible screening device had various outcomes. Research indicated that cultural differences as well as sex differences were found when using the KFD (Cabacungan, 1985). Generally, the exact nature of what the KFD measures was not clear.

Despite these limitations, the KFD showed promise as a tool that generated information about an individual's personality state. Research indicated that the KFD was a particularly useful instrument when evaluating children who were suspected sexual abuse survivors (Goodwin, 1982). Further evidence is needed to determine whether or not the KFD can adequately distinguish between other groups such as emotionally disturbed versus well-adjusted children. It is recommended that the KFD be used as a tool to gather information about a child's view of self in relationship to family members.

FAMILY-CENTERED CIRCLE DRAWINGS (1990)

Another useful instrument is the Family-Centered Circle Drawings (FCCD), developed by Burns (1990), which furnishes information on parent-self relationships. The FCCD differed from the KFD in that the therapist was able to see the client's relationship with one parent at a time and focused in on one particular symbol. This assessment seemed to be more helpful in uncovering the barriers in the client's past relationship with his or her parents as opposed to discovering or getting in touch with his or her inner parents.

Reliability and validity of the FCCD was not examined. Further, interpretation of the FCCD was limited. The FCCD was an interesting approach that generated information about the client's relationship with self and family; yet, the assessment lacked important data regarding administration requirements and interpretation. Guidelines for special populations such as learning disabled, hearing impaired, and culturally diverse individuals were not discussed. Overall, the FCCD has great potential as an art therapy assessment. With additional research information, the FCCD may be a valuable tool when viewing the client's relationship to herself and her family. The FCCD may be helpful in cases where the client has conflict with one or both parents. When working with sexual abuse survivors, I found that the symbols used were particularly helpful to clients who were struggling to remember parts of their past or make sense of their relationships with their parents or siblings.

HOUSE-TREE-PERSON TEST (1987)

The House-Tree-Person Test (HTP) was designed to provide information on personality attributes and interpersonal relationships. The HTP (Buck, 1987) utilized chromatic as well as achromatic drawings. Guidelines for interpretation were clearly outlined. Buck (1987) furnished case examples that illustrated the quantitative and qualitative scoring methods. The manual was very detailed in its approach to design, administration, scoring, and interpretation. The quantitative method of the test was complex and required additional time in determining scores.

Reliability and validity evidence has yet to be established for the HTP. Some interrater reliability evidence was provided by a few researchers (Marzolf & Kirchner, 1972). Validity evidence was mixed. Buck (1987) recommended that the HTP be used as a screening device to measure maladjustment, appraise personality integration, and identify common personality characteristics of a specific population; yet, he did not provide evidence that the HTP was a valid device for screening in these areas. Since the standardization sample was questionable, caution should be taken when using the HTP as a measure of intellectual functioning.

The case illustrations were helpful in providing insight on the use of the HTP. Another positive feature of this assessment was that it incorporated color, a factor neglected by some art therapy tests. Validity and reliability evidence needs to be established. It is recommended that the HTP be used as a tool to gather information on client issues rather than as a measure of intellectual functioning. The following assessment, while lacking validity and reliability evidence, has more clinical usefulness as compared to the HTP.

KINETIC HOUSE-TREE-PERSON TEST (1987)

Burns (1987) added a kinetic component to the HTP when designing the Kinetic House Tree Person Test (KHTP). He found that moving figures yielded more information about client issues as compared to static figures. Additionally, combining the house, tree, and person all on one page provided more information than when viewed separately. The manual was easy to read and contained several case examples to assist the therapist with interpretation. Another desirable feature of the KHTP was the incorporation of Maslow's (1954) theory to create a developmental model for the assessment. Burns (1987) modified Maslow's approach to interpret the items on the KHTP.

The KHTP may be difficult to interpret when a symbol occurs that was not included in the case examples or the summary tables. Although Burns (1987) provided a table for the scoring of attachments, he did not include scoring information when discussing the case examples. Despite the limitations, KHTP generated some valuable information about the client's perception of herself, her environment, and her family. The kinetic component was a valuable addition to the HTP. The interaction of the items as well as the developmental model were a strong improvement over the HTP. Overall, the manual was clear and the test was easy to administer. Although validity and reliability evidence has yet to be established, the KHTP may be a particularly useful test when working with new clients. In one drawing, the therapist will gain knowledge of the client's view of self in relationship to the environment and to the family. I use this assessment frequently when working with clients.

DIAGNOSTIC DRAWING SERIES (1986)

Cohen (1985) developed the Diagnostic Drawing Series (DDS) which measured behavioral and affective states of the client through structured and unstructured drawing tasks. One advantage of using the DDS was that three drawings were obtained in one session. Interpretation of the DDS may be difficult. Other than noting the presence or absence of pictorial characteristics, the handbook and rating guide did not provide information related to diagnostic categories. Another possible limitation was the time factor. The pressure of completing a drawing in 15 minutes may cause stress and anxiety in some people.

Research on the DDS, to date, has shown that it can distinguish between clinical populations and well-adjusted individuals. People with adjustment disorders, depression, dysthymia, schizophrenia, and organic syndromes had drawing styles characteristically different than well-adjusted individuals. Guidelines for the interpretation of the DDS with special populations was lacking. Overall, the DDS showed promise as tool to provide information on clinical diagnoses. More important, Cohen (1985) established reliability and validity of the DDS. This was another assessment that utilized color. I recommend the DDS when determining the status of individuals in need of clinical evaluations. Although research is lacking with respect to using the DDS with sexual abuse survivors, it has potential to yield clinical information that may be helpful in diagnosing posttraumatic stress disorder.

MAGAZINE PHOTO COLLAGE (1993)

The Magazine Photo Collage (MPC) was designed to reveal a client's conflicts, defense mechanisms, and styles of functioning. This approach evaluated collage images as opposed to drawing style. Landgarten (1993) designed a four-task assessment protocol that was simple to administer and fit into the treatment process easily. Interpretation was based on the client's free associations and the therapist's observation of the manner in which the collage was completed. Landgarten (1993) presented clear guidelines for the administration of the MPC, materials needed, and case examples. Additionally, the MPC appeared to counter some of the problems inherent in cross-cultural counseling by taking into consideration images familiar to clients with diverse backgrounds.

The MPC used only images of people and inanimate objects. This limited the scope of the assessment in that animal and nature images were not considered. The fact that the MPC was to be completed in one session may be limiting. Another shortcoming was that the tasks were viewed separately. With an assessment of this nature, common themes among the tasks should be noted. Interpretation of the tasks may be difficult. The exact nature of how the collage measured transference and countertransference issues was unclear. The same holds true for the interpretation of the client's attitude from one particular image. Additional information was needed on the interpretation of the collage tasks.

The MPC lacked validity and reliability evidence. Since Landgarten (1993) claimed that the MPC was a multicultural assessment, research should be completed to support this point. Overall, the MPC appeared to be an empowering approach when working with clients. It offered the client a choice in selection images and interpretation of the collage. Also, it reduced the possibility of cultural bias by including images consistent with a client's cultural background. The MPC may increase a client's awareness of self by yielding information about inner conflicts and relationships with others. It may be a useful tool for therapists engaged in cross-cultural counseling.

I have used the MPC when working with a group of sexual abuse survivors. Collage work was a powerful mode for working through feelings associated with the abuse. It was particularly useful for people who were threatened by drawing or felt inadequate. Selecting images can be just as powerful in revealing issues associated with abuse as are drawings. More importantly, the clients felt empowered through their collage work and were able to deal with boundary issues.

COGNITIVE ART THERAPY ASSESSMENT (1988)

Horovitz-Darby (1988) created the Cognitive Art Therapy Assessment (CATA) which combined drawing, painting, and clay. Validity and reliability evidence has not been established for the CATA. Although this assessment is not standardized, it does yield clinical information that may be helpful when working with sexual abuse issues. What is unique about this assessment is that it allows for the development of a theme in the client's art that may relate to clinical issues (Brooke, 1996). In my work with sexual abuse survivors, several themes have emerged through the use of this assessment: need for protection and defense, helplessness, need for nurturance, and feelings of loss.

SILVER DRAWING TEST (1990)

Silver (1990) designed the Silver Drawing Test (SDT) to assess cognitive abilities in three areas: sequential concepts, spatial concepts, and concept formation. The SDT was a creative attempt to measure cognitive skills in a nonverbal manner. Although comprehensive in its approach, the SDT had several weaknesses.

Reliability evidence was mixed. The largest problem with the SDT was the lack of evidence to support the claim that the instrument was a discriminator for depression. Since Silver (1990) did not attempt to furnish this evidence, the SDT should not be used as an indicator of depression. More importantly, there was no evidence of randomized samples. Since the demographics of the sample, particularly one's cultural background, were not discussed, it was difficult to determine how the results of the SDT generalize to other populations.

Validity evidence was found lacking for this instrument, particularly the subtests, Drawing from Observation and Predictive Drawing. Also, Silver (1990) neglected to establish validity evidence for the Emotional Projection section of the test. Generally, there was no evidence to indicate what the test measures or how well it does so. Horovitz (1996) stated that the emotional projection part of the assessment was revealing when working with sexual abuse survivors. Whales, brides, knives, and beds were just of the few images she observed when working with this population.

CONCLUSION

The assessments reviewed in this chapter represent only a few of the art therapy assessments available today. Some assessments have provided evidence that they are useful tools when working with sexual abuse survivors whereas other have the potential to be used in this area. Although many of the assessments lacked reliability and validity evidence, most demonstrated clinical usefulness. The next chapter will focus on possible indicators of sexual abuse utilizing some of the previous art therapy assessments.

REFERENCES

Brooke, S.: *Tools of the trade: A therapist's guide to art therapy assess-ments.* Springfield, IL, Charles C Thomas, 1996.

Buck, J.N.: *The House-Tree-Person Technique: Revised manual.* LosAngeles, Western Psychological Services, 1987.

Burns, R.C.: *A guide to family centered circle drawings.* New York, Brunner/Mazel, 1990.

Burns, R.C.: *Kinetic-House-Tree-Person-Drawings: An interpretive manual.* New York, Brunner/Mazel, 1987.

Burns, R.C., & Kaufman, S.H.: *Actions, styles, and symbols in Kinetic Family Drawings (K-F-D): An interpretive manual.* New York, Brunner/Mazel, 1972.

Cabacungan, L.F.: The child's representation of his family in Kinetic Family Drawings (KFD): A cross-cultural comparison. *Psychologia, 28*: 228-236, 1985.

Cohen, B.M. (Ed.): *The Diagnostic Drawing Series handbook.* Alexandria, VA, Barry Cohen, 1985.

Cummings, J.A.: An evaluation of an objective scoring system for the KFDs. *Dissertation Abstracts, 41(6-A)*: 2313, 1980.

Goodwin, J.: Use of drawings in evaluating children who may be incest victims. *Children and Youth Services Review, 4*: 269-278, 1982 .

Horovitz, E.: Personal interview with the Director of Art Therapy at Hillside Children's Center. May 15, 1996.

Horovitz-Darby, E.G.: Art therapy assessment of a minimally language skilled deaf child. Chapter 11 in *Mental Health Assessment of Deaf Clients: Special Conditions.* Proceedings from the 1988 University of California's Center on Deafness Conference, ADARA: 115-127, 1988.

Koppitz, E.M.: *Psychological evaluation of children's human figure drawings.* New York, Grune & Stratton, 1968.

Landgarten, H. B.: *Magazine photo collage.* New York, Brunner/Mazel, 1993.

Lingren, R.H.: An attempted replication of emotional indicators in human figure drawings by shy and aggressive children. *Psychological Reports, 29*: 35-38, 1971.

Marzolf, S.S., & Kirchner, J.H.: House-Tree-Person drawings and personality traits. *Journal of Personality Assessment, 36(2)*: 148-165, 1972.

Maslow, A.H.: *Motivation and personality.* New York, Harper & Row, 1954.

McPhee, J., & Wegner, K.: Kinetic-Family-Drawing styles and emotionally disturbed childhood behavior. *Journal of Personality Assessment, 40*: 487-491, 1976.

Mostkoff, D.L., & Lazarus, P.J.: The Kinetic Family Drawing: The reliability of an objective scoring system. *Psychology in the Schools, 20*: 16-20, 1983.

Motta, R.W.; Little, S.G., & Tobin, M.I.: The use and abuse of human figure drawings. *School Psychology Quarterly, 8(3)*: 162-169, 1993.

Naglieri, J.A.; McNeish, T.J., & Bardos, A.N.: *Draw a Person: Screening Procedure for Emotional Disturbance.* Austin, Pro-Ed, 1991.

Norford, B.C., & Barakat, L.P.: The relationship of human figure drawings to aggressive behavior in preschool children. *Psychology in the Schools, 27*: 318-325, 1990.

Silver, R.: *Silver Drawing Test of Cognitive Skills and Adjustment.* Sarasota, FL, Ablin Press, 1990.

Chapter 3

GRAPHIC INDICATORS
OF SEXUAL ABUSE

There has been little research which has focused on graphic indicators. However, numerous observations have been made by art therapists, psychotherapists, and other mental health practitioners. "The use of art expression has allowed us to explore our hypothesis that sexually exploited children may produce predictable themes and images through their art and that substantiation of this hypothesis might aid greatly in the identification and treatment of victims " (Carozza & Hiersteiner, 1982, p. 167). This chapter will concentrate on common images in the drawings of child and adult survivors of sexual abuse. Although the intent is to identify possible victims of abuse, the significance of indicators is questioned by some practitioners, primarily due to the fact that identification of indicators is based on case studies rather than research studies. Additionally, many of the observations were made by non art therapists. Identification of graphic indicators is in the beginning stages. Common images have emerged in the literature. The value of identifying common images is that drawings may aid in the disclosure of aspects of the sexual abuse (Kelley, 1985; Burgess, 1988).

HUMAN FIGURE DRAWINGS

Human figures drawn by sexual abuse survivors often have recurring themes. Omission of body parts is common in the artwork of sexual abuse survivors, such as missing hands and feet (Kelley, 1984; Sidun & Rosenthal, 1987; Burgess, 1988; Jones, 1989; Malchiodi, 1990; Riordan & Verdel, 1991; Burgess & Hartman, 1993; Chantler et al., 1993; Sadowski & Loesch, 1993). Spring (1988) conducted a research study with female, adult survivors and observed fragmented bodies in their art. Some sexually-abused clients will portray figures with very detailed emphasis on the face and clothing of the upper portion while neglecting to represent the lower portion of the body (Malchiodi, 1990; Sadowski & Loesch, 1993). This may represent helplessness or lack of support related to the sexual abuse (Klepsch & Logie, 1982; Sadowski & Loesch, 1993). For those survivors who do not draw the lower portion, Spring (1996) observed that this may be a fear of acknowledging the weapon of sexual abuse if it was the penis. Spring stated that this depends on the identification of the figure, whether it represents the self or the perpetrator. I have noticed that the focus for some survivors is on intellect rather than affect, which associated with the body; therefore, some tend to draw only portraits. Malchiodi (1990) attributed the lack of torso to denying the sexual areas of the body.

> We can, therefore, surmise that the absent torsos were not the result of cognitive limitations. Alice's omission is clearly related to her sexual victimization and points to her use of denial. She uses this primitive defense mechanism in an attempt to keep unconscious the painful experience to which she was subjected. (Kaufman & Wohl, 1992, p. 55)

Some researchers have noted that the absence of body parts indicated denial (Carozza & Hiersteiner, 1982; Levick 1983). Separation of trunk may also reveal sexual abuse (Kaufman and Wohl, 1992). Generally, drawings by survivors depict poorly integrated figures (Stember, 1980; DiLeo, 1983; Hibbard & Hartman, 1990; Chantler et al., 1993).

According to Kelley (1984), a registered nurse working with children, shading of the figure suggests preoccupation, fixation, and anxiety. Signs of anxiety in children can take other forms, according to Briggs and Lehmann (1989): omissions, distortions, heavy lines, turned-down mouth, raised arms, and arms turned inward.

Explicit depiction of genitals by children has been used as an indicator of abuse by some clinicians (Kelley, 1984; Yates et al., 1985; Miller et al., 1987; Hibbard et al., 1987; Burgess, 1988; Faller, 1988; Hibbard & Hartman, 1990; Hagood, 1993).

> It must be cautioned that, although the presence of genitalia in a child's drawing should alert one to consider the possibility of sexual abuse, it does not prove it, just as the absence of genitalia does not exclude abuse.(Hibbard, et. al., 1987, p. 129)

Kelley (1984) found that sexually-abused children shade the genital and chest areas of figures. Exaggeration or minimalization of sexual features was also widespread in children's art products (Yates et al., 1985; Riordan & Verdel, 1991; Chantler et al., 1993; Dufrene, 1994; Cohen-Liebman, 1995). Sexual connotation in children's artwork can take other forms such as depicting figures wearing sexy clothing or make-up, or with long eye-lashes that conveys seductiveness (Howard & Jakab, 1968; Malchiodi, 1990). On the other hand, some children may avoid sexualization, thus, creating figures with ambiguous sexuality (Kelley, 1984; Faller, 1988). With male survivors whose perpetrator was also male, I have observed that gender confusion or questions about sexual identity may surface in their artwork. Additionally, I have found that facial features sometimes have female connotations for some male survivors.

Other themes include the lack of a mouth which may relate the the secrecy surrounding the abuse; this was observed in the art of children and adolescents (Briggs & Lehmann, 1985; Sidun & Rosenthal, 1987). Huge circular mouths are often drawn by children when oral sex was involved (Briggs & Lehmann, 1985). Spring (1993) felt that the circular mouth may be related to the silent scream. Riordan and Verdel (1991) found both the emphasis on the mouth and the omission of the mouth in the work of child survivors. Drachnik (1994) noted that some sexually abused children have drawn protruding tongues in their art; yet, this graphic indicator has not been empirically validated.

Spring (1988) found that sexually-abused adults were more likely to draw eyes. Her research study utilized 225 drawings and included a control group. The survivors included two groups: 15 rape victims and 15 women who experienced multiple sexual abuse incidents. All 30 women were diagnosed with posttraumatic stress disorder. Their drawings were compared to a control group of 15 women who did not experience sexual abuse or other life-threatening events or illnesses. Spring (1988) associated the disembodied eye, highly stylized eye, or tearful eye to guilt within the context of sexual abuse. Earlier literature in the field revealed an association between eyes and sexuality or sexual abuse (Dax, 1953; Howard & Jakab, 1969; Nederlander, 1977; Hammer, 1978; Stember, 1978; & Garrett & Ireland, 1979).

Low self-concept may be a characteristic of sexual abuse survivors. One way that low self-concept is graphically portrayed is by representing the self as a small figure. DiLeo (1983) supported the view that small figures drawn at or near the lower edge of the paper indicated feelings of inadequacy, insecurity, and even depression. Hibbard and Hartman (1990) reported that sexually-abused children will draw tiny figures more often that nonabused children, which they credited to shyness or withdrawal.

Kaufman and Wohl (1992) observed that some sexual abuse survivors will often shade hair heavily, possibly revealing difficulty controlling impulses. Although other others have not made mention of this fact, Kaufman and Wohl (1992) related thinning hair at the top of the head to possible sexual abuse.

Clown images sometimes characterized the work of child survivors (Burgess & Holmstrom, 1979; Stember, 1980; Hagood, 1993). "This concealment device often appears among severely traumatized female victims who are maintaining a facade of smiling exuberance" (Kelley, 1984, p. 424). Although abused girls depict more clown images, sexually-abused boys also depict concealment through football helmets, sports equipment, or other protective gear. Kaufman and Wohl (1992) found that abused girls were significantly identified more often than abused boys using human figure drawings.

Chase (1987) examined human figure drawings of 34 female incest survivors, ranging in age from 5 to 16, with a matched sample of 26 emotionally-disturbed subjects and 34 subjects with no history of sexual abuse or emotional disturbance. When compared with the emotionally-disturbed subjects, sexually-abused children significantly drew more hands omitted, fingers omitted, clothing omitted, and presence of phallic-like objects. When compared to nonabused children, sexually-abused subjects significantly drew large circular eyes, mouth emphasized, long neck, arms omitted, hands omitted, fingers omitted, clothing omitted, and presence of phallic-like objects.

FAMILY DRAWINGS

The Kinetic Family Drawing (KFD) has revealed several common themes in the artwork of sexual abuse survivors. Kaufman and Wohl (1992) found that the KFD significantly identified male and female survivors of sexual abuse. Goodwin (1982) reported evidence of isolation, role reversals, and encapsulation in the KFD's of child survivors. Cohen and Phelps (1985) discovered that the child will often omit self from the KFD. In my work with adult survivors, omission of self was common, especially if the person was struggling to remember aspects of the traumatic situation. Burgess and Hartman (1990; 1993) found that the KFD may reveal family conflicts. Isolation, barriers, encapsulation, and sexual themes were also portrayed in the KFD's of children and adolescents (Johnston, 1970; German, 1986). Encapsulation and compartmentalization were repetitive features in KFD's of sexually-abused children (Kaufman & Wohl, 1992). "The omission of the trunk and appendages in these family members is important since these are instruments of power with which to manipulate or be manipulated" (Wohl & Kaufman, 1985, p.74).

Goodwin (1982) used the KFD when evaluating possible sexual abuse survivors. Although she implemented a series of drawings in the evaluation, only the KFD will be discussed. She examined 19 female children who were suspected sexual abuse survivors. Goodwin (1982) found evidence of isolation, compartmentalization, and role reversals in the drawings of sexual abuse survivors. Additionally, she observed that these children drew themselves larger than their mother.

Chase (1987) compared the KFD's of 27 female incest survivors, ranging in ages from 5 to 16, with a matched sample of 37 emotionally-disturbed children and 37 subjects with no history of sexual abuse or emotional disturbance. When compared to the emotionally-disturbed sample, incest survivors significantly drew encapsulated figures. When compared to the nonabused sample, survivors significantly depicted nurturance of self and mother.

Kaplan (1991) examined the drawings of 51 males and 54 females ranging in age from 7 to 14 years. Thirty-five children were sexually-abused, 35 emotionally-disturbed, and 35 were "normal" children. Three objective raters identified the presence of designated graphic features in the drawings. The two most significant indicators were the "family engaged in sexual activity," and "family engaged in intimate activity."

Hackbarth (1991) and colleagues found that the KFD significantly differentiated between abused and nonabused children. Thirty children, ranging in age from 6 to 13 years, classified as sexually-abused by the Department of Human Services were compared to 30 unidentified children in a public school district. They ranged in age from 6 to 11 years. The subjects were matched with those in the experimental group: 25 girls and 5 boys (26 were white and 4 were African American). Mothers also completed the KFD. Using the Like to Live in Family (LLIF) rating procedure (Burns, 1982), five counselors scored the KFDs on desirability of family life. sexually-abused children drew significantly less desirable family situations compared to their mothers. Mothers of sexually-abused children drew significantly less desirable family settings than did mothers of unidentified children. Mothers and their unidentified children did not significantly differ in their KFDs. "The KFD shows enough promise as an evaluation tool in the area of sexual abuse that elementary counselors may want to consider this instrument for inclusion in their repertoire of assessment skills" (Hackbarth et al., 1991, p. 260).

HOUSE DRAWINGS

Some clinicians have discovered that red houses are sometimes drawn by child survivors (Silvercloud, 1982; Cohen & Phelps, 1985; Hagood, 1994). Also, children who were sexually-abused tend to omit bedrooms or if bedrooms are present, indicate bizarre sleeping arrangements or lack of privacy (Goodwin, 1982). One window treated differently on a house or crossed out windows may be possible indicators of childhood sexual abuse, as observed by some clinicians (Silvercloud, 1982; Hagood, 1994; Cohen & Phelps, 1985; Kaufman & Wohl, 1992). The inclusion of circles, in general, was also another possible indicator (Sidun & Rosenthal, 1987). According to Horovitz (1996), red curtains and/or doors were depicted in the drawings of child and adolescent survivors.

TREE DRAWINGS

Kaufman and Wohl (1992) conducted a pilot study with 54 children, 18 identified survivors of sexual abuse, 18 children from a mental health organization, and 18 children randomly drawn from the community. They discovered that tree drawings significantly identified male survivors of sexual abuse as compared to females. "The later may be clinically valid when we understand that the tree, as a growing vegetative form, may at some level relate to the "growing" shape of the erect penis and that the injury to a male's sense of his virility may be unconsciously connected to the tree" (Kaufman & Wohl, 1992, p. 34). Additionally, Kaufman and Wohl observed that younger children, 4 to 6 years, were significantly identified using the tree portion of the HTP as compared to older children, 7 to 10 years. Generally, the separation of the trunk from the crown, dead trees, and absence of leaves characterized the tree drawings of abused children. In my work with adult sexual abuse survivors, I found that many drew slanted trees (Brooke, 1995).

HEART IMAGES

Jones (1989) noted that survivors tend to draw encapsulated hearts. According to Malchiodi (1990), sexually-abused girls will use heart images in their artwork. This may take the form of the traditional, stereotyped, heart images or using hearts in shapes on clothing, lips, or hair (Malchiodi, 1990).

> A suffering child is perhaps instinctively drawn to the sacrificial heart. The sacrifice of the innocent may be an archetypal memory of children. (Kidd & Wix, 1996, p. 110)

When working with a group of sexual abuse survivors, heart images were commonly depicted (Brooke, 1995). Some survivors often depict broken hearts, which includes wedges as the dividing line, an image that Spring (1993) found when working with adult survivors. Jones (1989) found the predominate use of hearts revealed that "something important is missing in their (children's) lives and that they wish this element could be present" (p. 180). Kaufman and Wohl (1992) reported that heart images reflected feelings of being exposed and vulnerable. Sagar (1990) discussed the case of Fay, a six-year-old, sexually-abused girl who made a clay figure that was given a heart transplant. It was important for her to do this before the patient died. "The heart, generally recognized as the seat of feelings, or the generator of feelings, if damaged or absent, would feel like death emotionally" (Sagar in Case & Dalley, 1990, p. 111)

ADDITIONAL DRAWING CHARACTERISTICS

The depiction of inclement weather may be indicative of childhood abuse (Stember, 1980; Manning, 1987; Miller et al., 1987) and depression (Urban, 1963). These pictures will often contain images of darkened skies and sun, heavy shading, and rain (Burgess, 1988). I have related turbulent weather to the perception of the environment as threatening. Clouds, particularly over human figures, have been associated with sexual abuse (Kaufman & Wohl, 1992). Movement, such as strong wind, was indicative of loss of control (Jolles, 1971; Manning, 1987):

> It has been observed that children who are in trouble frequently produce more moving art than children who are well behaved. Particularly during periods when the struggle for control is intense, art often becomes meager, overly pious, or saccharin, or the child loses interest. (Kramer, 1971, p. 152)

Favorite weather drawings made by child survivors have revealed insecurity and isolation of affect (Burgess & Hartman, 1993). Generally, drawings by child survivors will show kinetic activity such as scribbling, dots, and violent themes (Jones, 1989).

Another possible indicator of childhood sexual abuse was enclosure or encapsulation of figures (Stember, 1978; Cohen & Phelps, 1985). Malchiodi (1990) defined encapsulation as anything in which the child has visually enclosed herself, such a house, a car, or a tree. DiLeo (1983) suggested that encapsulation expressed feelings of isolation and lack of communication. Floating images and lack of a ground line may reveal a chaotic social environment and an attempt to compensate (Carozza & Hiersteiner, 1982). Spring (1993) related floating images, such as balloons, to dissociation.

On a more abstract level, circles and wedges were often represented in the art of sexually-abused people (Spring, 1985; Sidun & Rosenthal, 1987; Malchiodi, 1990; Dufrene, 1994; Cohen-Liebman, 1995). Spring (1985; 1988) found that wedges, for adult survivors, symbolized feelings of being threatened in the past as well as the present.

Color has also been related to the identification of sexual abuse survivors. Malchiodi (1990) noted that survivors tend to use complementary colors, such as red and green, which make it difficult to look at a drawing for any length of time. Additionally, black and red are common colors used by sexual abuse survivors (Cohen & Phelps, 1985; Spring, 1978, 1993). I can remember the first time that I led an art therapy group for sexual abuse survivors. As we were beginning the first exercise, group members complained that there were not enough dark colors, particularly black.

SUMMARY

Given that sexual abuse is difficult to talk about, particularly child survivors, mental health practitioners are focusing on additional measures for identifying possible victims, such as graphic indicators of abuse. "sexually-abused children use art materials symbolically to express feelings of being full of mess inside, of being messed-up, and of trying to find some way to control and handle the mess or poison" (Sagar, in Case & Dalley, 1990, p. 108). Art therapy provides a visual dialogue to communicate feelings without relying on words.

Common themes have been noted in the literature: Drawing tiny figures, omission of body parts, encapsulated figures, hearts, circles, wedges, eyes, and drawings which show kinetic activity. The debate about sexual abuse indicators stems from the fact that a majority of the literature focuses on clinical observations of case studies. Also, some clinicians were not art therapists. There has been only one empirical research study (Spring, 1988). A few studies cited in this chapter did conduct research that will begin to establish validity for some graphic indicators of sexual abuse (Cohen & Phelps, 1985; Chase, 1987; Hackbarth e. al., 1991; Kaplan, 1991; Kaufman & Wohl, 1992; Spring, 1988). Although the identification of graphic indicators is only in the beginning stages, the use of drawings with sexual abuse survivors is still recommended over other measurement approaches (Bybee, 1987).

Clinicians should be aware of the "normal" stages of artistic development (Malchiodi, 1994). It is beyond the scope of this text to discuss stages of artistic development. When I conduct art therapy diagnostic assessments, I use Lowenfeld and Brittain's (1987) stages of development for a comparison. Additional sources include Kellogg (1969) and Gardner (1980).

It is important to stress that therapists should not determine abuse from one drawing. It is my opinion that a battery of assessments should be used when sexual abuse is suspected. Using several evaluations, Burgess (1988) found sexually-abused children differed significantly from nonabused children as far as shading, omission of body parts, and sexualization of figures. Given that many assessments have weaknesses, especially in the areas of reliability and validity, a battery would provide more information and allow for the emergence of themes that yield clinical information (Brooke, 1996).

REFERENCES

Briggs, F., & Lehmann, K.: Significance of children's drawings in cases of sexual abuse. *Early Child Development and Care, 47*: 131-147, 1989.

Brooke, S.L.: Art therapy: An approach to working with sexual abuse survivors. *The Arts in Psychotherapy, 22(5)*: 447-466, 1995.

Brooke, S.: *Tools of the trade: A therapist's guide to art therapy assessments.* Springfield, IL, Charles C Thomas, 1996.

Burgess, E.J.: Sexually-abused children and their drawings. *Archives of Psychiatric Nursing, 2(2)*: 65-73, 1988.

Burgess, A.W., & Hartman, C.R.: Children's drawings. *Child Abuse & Neglect, 17*: 161-168, 1993.

Burgess, A.W., & Holmstrom, L.L.: *Rape: Crisis and recovery.* Bowie, MD, Robert J. Brady Co, 1979.

Burns, R.C.: *Kinetic-House-Tree-Person-Drawings: An interpretive manual.* New York, Brunner/Mazel, 1987.

Bybee, D.: *Measurement issues in child sexual abuse.* Paper presented at the Biennial Meeting for the Society for Research in Child Development. Baltimore, MD, April 23-26, 1987.

Carozza, P.M., & Heirsteiner, C.L.: Young female incest victims in treatment: Stages of growth seen with a group art therapy model. *Clinical Social Work Journal, 10(3)*: 165-175, 1982.

Case, C., & Dalley, T.: *Working with children in art therapy.* New York, Travistock/ Routledge, 1990.

Chantler, L., Pelco, L., & Mertin, P.: The psychological evaluation of child sexual abuse using the Louisville Behavior Checklist and Human Figure Drawing. *Child Abuse & Neglect, 17*: 271-279, 1993.

Chase, D.A.: An analysis of human figure and kinetic family drawings of sexually-abused children and adolescents. *Dissertation Abstracts International, 48(2)*: 338, 1987.

Cohen, F.W., & Phelps, R.E.: Incest markers in children's artwork. *Arts in Psychotherapy, 12*: 265-284, 1985.

Cohen-Liebman, M.S.: Drawings as judiciary aids in child sexual abuse litigation: A composite list of indicators. *The Arts in Psychotherapy, 22(5)*: 475-483, 1995.

Dax, C.E.: *Experimental studies in psychiatric art.* London, Faber & Faber, Limited, 1953.

DiLeo, J.H.: *Interpreting children's drawings.* New York, Brunner/Mazel, 1983.

Drachnik, C.: The tongue as a graphic symbol of sexual abuse. *Art Therapy: Journal of American Art Therapy Association, 11(1)*: 58-61, 1994.

Dufrene, P.: Art therapy and the sexually-abused child. *Art Education, November.* 6-11, 1994.

Faller, K.: *Child sexual abuse: An interdisciplinary manual for diagnosis case management and treatment.* New York, Columbia University Press, 1988.

Gardner, H.: *Artful scribbles: The significance of children's drawings.* New York, Basic Books, 1980.

Garrett, C., & Ireland, M.: A therapeutic art session with rape victims. *American Journal of Art Therapy, 18*: 103-106, 1979.

German, D.: *The female adolescent incest victim: Personality, self-esteem, and family orientation.* Unpublished doctoral dissertation, Andrews University. Cited in Handler & Habenicht, (1994), 1986.

Goodwin, J.: Use of drawings in evaluating children who may be incest victims. *Children and Youth Services Review, 4*: 269-278, 1982.

Hackbarth, S.G.; Murphy, H.D., and McQuary, J.P.: Identifying sexually-abused children by using Kinetic Family Drawings. *Elementary School Guidance & Counseling, 25*: 225-260, 1991.

Hagood, M.M.: Diagnosis or dilemma: Drawings of sexually-abused children. Art Therapy: *Journal of the American Art Therapy Association, 11(1)*: 37-42, 1994.

Hammer, E.: *The Clinical Application of Projective Drawings.* Springfield, IL, Charles C Thomas, 1978.

Handler, L., & Habenicht, D.: The Kinetic Family Drawing technique: A review of the literature. *Journal of Personality Assessment, 62(3)*: 440-464, 1994.

Hibbard, R.A., & Hartman, G.L.: Emotional indicators in human figure drawings of sexually victimized and nonabused children. *Journal of Clinical Psychology, 46 (2)*: 211-219, 1990.

Hibbard, R.A., Roghmann, K., & Hoekelman, R.A.: Genitalia in children's drawings: An association with sexual abuse. *Pediatrics, 79(1)*, 129-137, 1987.

Horovitz, E.: Personal interview with the Director of Art Therapy at Hillside Children's Center. May 15, 1996.

Howard, M.C., & Jakab, I.: *Psychiatry and art: Volume 2 8th International Colloquium Psychopathology of Expression.* New York, Basel, 1968.

Johnston, M.S.K.: The sexually mistreated child: Diagnostic evaluation. *Child Abuse & Neglect, 3*: 943-951, 1979.

Jones, L.A.: Hearts wish. *Early Child Development and Care, 42*: 175-182, 1989.

Kaplan, B.J.: Graphic indicators of sexual abuse in drawings of sexually abused, emotionally-disturbed children, and nondisturbed children: child sexual abuse. *Dissertation Abstracts International, 52(2)*: 1065, 1991.

Kaufman, B., & Wohl, A.: *Casualties of childhood: A developmental perspective on sexual abuse using projective drawings.* New York, Brunner/Mazel, 1992.

Kelley, S.J.: The use of art therapy with sexually-abused children. *Journal of Psychosocial Nursing, 22(12)*: 12-18, 1984.

Kelley, S.J.: Drawings: Critical communications for sexually-abused children. *Pediatric Nursing, 11*: 1985.

Kellogg, R.: *Analyzing children's art.* Mountain View, CA, Hayfield, 1969.

Kidd, J., & Wix, L.: Images of the heart: Archetypal imagery in the therapeutic art work. Art Therapy: *Journal of the American Art Therapy Association, 13(2)*: 108-113, 1996.

Klepsch, M., & Logie, L.: *Children draw and tell: An introduction to the projective uses of children's human figure drawings.* New York, Brunner/Mazel, 1982.

Kramer, E.: *Art as therapy with children.* New York, Schocken Books, 1971.

Levick, M: *They could not talk and so they drew.* Springfield, IL, Charles C Thomas, 1983.

Lowenfeld, V., & Brittain, W.L. (1987). *Creative and Mental Growth.* (8th ed.). New York, Macmillan, 1987.

Malchiodi, C.A.: *Comparative study of the DAP and the Life Size Body Drawing in the assessment of child abuse.* Proceedings of the 18th Annual Conference of the American Art Therapy Association. Mundelein, IL, AATA, Inc, 1987.

Malchiodi, C.A.: *Breaking the silence: Art therapy with children from violent homes.* New York, Brunner/Mazel, 1990.

Malchiodi, C.A.: *Using drawings in the assessment of children from violent homes.* Speech presented at the National Children's Mental Health Conference, Jacksonville, FL, 1994.

Manning, T.M. (1987). Aggression depicted in abused children's drawings. *Arts in Psychotherapy, 14*, 15-24.

Miller, T.W., Veltkamp, L.J., & Janson, D.: Projective measures in the clinical evaluation of sexually-abused children. *Child Psychiatry and Human Development, 18(1)*: 47-57, 1987.

Nederlander, C.: The use of graphic expression in the modification of sexual behavior. *American Journal of Art Therapy, 16*: 61-77, 1977.

Riordan, R.J., & Verdel, A.C.: Evidence of sexual abuse in children's art products. *The School Counselor, 39*: 116-121, 1991.

Sadowski, P.M., & Loesch, L.C.: Using children's drawings to detect potential child sexual abuse. *Elementary School Guidance & Counseling, 28*: 115-123, 1993.

Sidun, N.M., & Rosenthal, R.H.: Graphic indicators of sexual abuse in Draw-A-Person tests of psychiatrically hospitalized adolescents. *The Arts in Psychotherapy, 14*: 25-33, 1987.

Silvercloud, B.: *Using art to express the unspeakable: A tool for intervention and therapy with the sexually-abused.* The proceedings of the Thirteenth Annual Conference of the American Art Therapy Association, Philadelphia, 1982.

Spring, D.: Jane, case of a rape victim rehabilitated by art therapy. In *Imagery: Its many dimensions and applications.* New York, Plenum Press, 1978.

Spring, D.: Sexual abuse and post-traumatic stress reflected in artistic symbolic language. *Dissertation Abstracts International, 50(80)*, 3716, 1988.

Spring, D.: Sexual abuse and post-traumatic stress reflected in artistic symbolic language. Author. 1-157, 1988.

Spring, D.: Shattered Images: The phenomenological language of sexual trauma. Chicago, IL, Magnolia Press, 1993.

Stember, C.J.: Art therapy: A new use in the diagnosis and treatment of sexually-abused children. In U.S. Department of Health and Human Services, Sexual Abuse of Children Selected Readings (pp 59-63). Washington, DC, US Government Printing Office, 1980.

Wohl, A., & Kaufman, B.: Silent screams and hidden Cries: An interpretation of artwork by children from violent homes. New York, Brunner/Mazel, 1985.

Yates, A., Beutler, L.E., & Crago, M.: Drawings by child victims of incest. Child Abuse and Neglect, 9: 183-189, 1985.

Chapter 4

MEMORIES OF SEXUAL ABUSE

NATURE OF MEMORY

One of the lectures that I present in my General Psychology course is on memory. Although there are a variety of definitions, I describe memory in terms of information processing: Memory is composed of interrelated components called storages (sensory, short, and long term). Myers (1996) defined memory as the persistence of learning over time through storage and retrieval of information.

> Memory images are a reconstruction of a past perception. They may be quite dim, almost nonsensory in nature, or may be extremely distinct, even projected on blank spaces, such as walls or papers, in an effort to localize them externally. (Laidlaw et al., 1990, p. 166-167)

Remembering data first involves acquiring and encoding the information. Next, the data is retained and stored. Last, information is retrieved. I teach my students about the three types of memory: recognition (identification of previously learned material), recall (retrieval of information learned earlier), and reconstruction (recounting past experience). The type of memory will influence the retrieval process. Additionally, memories are dependent on context or mood. "Memory is now regarded as a dynamic and highly plastic process, never independent of present time and never independent of present context" (Brenneis, 1994, p. 1031).

Fredrickson (1992) outlined five types of memory. Recall memory, a process for the conscious mind, is a retained memory of events accompanied by the sense of having experienced those events. This type of memory requires cognitive maturation. Although Hewitt (1994) found that infants are capable of remembering preverbal experiences, researchers have found that these memories may be unreliable (Loftus, 1993; Myers, 1996). Abuse that happens before cognitive maturation, usually two years of age or under, entails unconscious forms of memory such as imaginistic, feeling, bodily, and acting-out memories. Imaginistic memory employs visual images, much like a slide show. Feeling memories are the emotional reactions to particular situations. Bodily memories record the kinesthetic responses to events. Ware (1995) defined body memories as "preverbal and averbal memory traces, that is to say, unspecific coenaesthetic memories sensed in the depths of a person's bowels and body tissue" (p. 5). Last, acting-out memories are spontaneous reenactments involving a verbal or bodily act in reaction to an event that is a reminder of the original episode. Unusual, repetitive behavior patterns or sensory experiences have been associated with early, sometimes forgotten, traumatic events (Dewald, 1989; Brenneis, 1994).

Given the wealth of information on the nature of memory, books could be written on the topic. It is beyond the scope of this text to present a detailed account of the nature of memory in humans. Generally, this chapter will provide basic information on forgetting of traumatic memories, "false memories," and retrieval strategies. Finally, the chapter will conclude with a discussion of the effectiveness of art therapy in working with memories of sexual abuse.

FORGETTING TRAUMATIC MEMORIES

In a discussion of memory, Freud (1937) stated that "all of the essentials are preserved; even things that seem completely forgotten are present somehow and somewhere, and have merely been buried and made inaccessible to the subject" (p. 260; cited in Brenneis, 1994). Forgetting of childhood sexual abuse, due to repression, blocking, or amnesia, is a characteristic of survivors (Emerson, 1988; Siegel & Romig, 1988; Blume, 1990; Ratican, 1992; Roland, 1993). Lack of access to memories of sexual abuse is generally associated with young age at the time of victimization, violent abuse, and extended duration of abuse (Williams, 1992; Briere & Conte, 1993; Ernsdorff & Loftus, 1993; Simonds, 1994; Enns et al., 1995). Terr (1994) argued that although young children may not verbally recall sexual abuse, they may retain behavioral or nonverbal memories, and engage in acting-out of the original trauma which is in line with Fredrickson's (1992) thinking the different types of memory. Yapko (1993) warned that even if a client cannot remember aspects of the past, therapists should not automatically assume memories are repressed.

Sexual abuse survivors are described as suffering from distortions of memory such as dissociative amnesia, dissociative fugue, dissociative identity disorder and depersonalization disorder (APA, 1994). Dissociation was defined as the splitting off from consciousness ideas that were bizarre, frightening, or inconsistent with the person's identity (Davies & Frawley, 1994). Generally, dissociation was described as "a disruption in the usually integrated functions of consciousness, memory, identity, or perception of the environment" (APA, 1994, p. 477). Also, it involves altering perception of the traumatic event (Chu & Dill, 1990; Spray, 1994). According to Spray (1994), dissociative memory is layered in a horizontal fashion and is stored in an area of the conscious mind. There is a considerable debate as to whether amnesia about childhood sexual abuse should be referred to as repression or dissociation.

Repression was defined as intentional or motivated forgetting of events that would cause internal conflict in the person (Freud, 1957; Bowers, 1990; Kihlstrom & Hoyt, 1990; Myers, 1996). According to Fredrickson (1992), sexual abuse memories are sometimes repressed by survivors. She defined repression as "a useful and necessary tool that unburdens your mind, leaving you free to focus your conscious energy on the here and now" (p. 22). Further, she asserted that repressed memories relate to abuse, sexual abuse, moreso than physical or emotional abuse. Fredrickson described the repressed memory syndrome as consisting of four categories (p. 41):

1. attractions, fears, or avoidances unexplained by known history;
2. indications of emerging memories;
3. evidence of disassociation;
4. time loss or memory blanks

Flashbacks, common household items, bodily sensations, and dreams are just a few of the triggers for repressed memories. Additionally, she stated that repressed memories involve elements of hypnosis in that children react to the sexual abuse by going into a trance state that allows them to become distant from the situation. According to Spray (1994), repressed "memory is layered vertically and memories are forced down into the unconscious where they cannot be accessed by the individual" (p. 6).

Many debate the use of repression to describe childhood sexual abuse (Ernsdorff & Loftus, 1993; Loftus, 1993; Ceci & Loftus, 1994): "Indeed, repression is almost surely overused as an explanation of memory failure, with normal forgetting, deliberate avoidance, intentional overfocusing, and infantile amnesia providing both more prosaic and parsimonious explanations of encoding and/or retrieval problems" (Ceci & Loftus, 1994, p. 352). Many practitioners prefer the use of disassociation to repression because trauma is often not related to internal conflicts: Dissociation more accurately conceptualizes the alterations of consciousness associated with sexual abuse and it occurs when typical defenses are not adequate (Briere, 1992; Davies & Frawley, 1994). "In the case of dissociation, individuals learn to divide attention in stressful situations, and in the case of repression, the person learns to divert attention from unpleasant cognitive and emotional events" (Enns et al., 1995, p. 220).

The debate over these terms may continue for quite some time. Theorists who use both terms argue that disassociation is an organizing or umbrella principle for understanding alterations of consciousness (Courtois, 1988; Terr, 1994). Terr (1994) asserted that victims of sexual abuse will use repression in early stages of abuse. As maturation progresses, the child will develop dissociation skills. The following two studies will illustrate both sides of the debate.

Williams (1994) examined 129 women with a previously documented history of sexual abuse 17 years earlier. She found that 38 percent of the women did not recall the abuse. Although some attributed the findings to denial or embarrassment (Loftus & Ketcham, 1994), Williams (1994) reported that these women volunteered information on other private, sexual matters without hesitation. Contrary to other findings (Herman & Schatzow, 1987; Briere & Conte, 1993; Loftus et al., 1994), Williams (1994) found that the ability to recall childhood sexual abuse was not related to physical force, sexual penetration, or genital trauma. Specifically, forgetting was related to young age and perpetration by a family member as opposed to a stranger.

Loftus and her colleagues (1994) examined recollection of childhood sexual abuse in a sample of 105 women being treated for substance abuse. Fifty-four percent of the women reported a history of childhood sexual abuse. Of that sample, 81 percent remembered all or part of the abuse their whole lives, whereas 19 percent reported that they forgot the abuse for a period of time and the memories returned later. It is not known what percentage of this sample was unable to recall any memories. Additionally, the results of a clinical population, substance abusers in this case, cannot be expected to generalize to the larger population.

Both studies have methodological weaknesses. Although additional research is needed, examination of traumatic memory has ethical as well as methodological dilemmas (Spring, 1996). Research does show that forgetting of traumatic memories occurs in some individuals. As a result, some clinicians have specialized in the retrieval of traumatic memories in order to help the person heal. The following section will discuss some of these strategies.

MEMORY RETRIEVAL

Some researchers have commented that many people enter therapy unaware that they were victims of childhood sexual abuse (Wolf & Alpert, 1991; Kuppersmith; 1992, Brenneis, 1994). As a result, some therapists began to specialize in the recovery of sexual abuse memories. Recovered memory therapy entails assisting clients to retrieve repressed memories of childhood sexual abuse in order to deal with current emotional or behavioral problems (Spray, 1994).

Access to difficult memories may be limited by psychological defenses as well as the nature of encoding. Trauma may be encoded by the more primitive, visually-based memory during times of stress. Also, access to traumatic memories may be dependent on the similarity of the sensory stimuli (Johnson, 1987; Howard, 1989). Flashbacks, dreams, and other visual stimuli may trigger memories of sexual abuse. "While flashbacks may appear to be random, often they are triggered by a 'traumatic associational clue' in the form of a sensory experience (sight, sound, smell, task, touch) or an even that literally or symbolically related to the original abuse" (Zeig, 1994, p. 412). Some researchers feel that flashbacks or dream content represent exact replicas of the original trauma (van der Kolk et al., 1984; Johnson, 1987). In an effort to retrieve blocked memories, a variety of techniques have been used to help survivors of sexual abuse.

According to Fredrickson (1992), repressed memories of child sexual abuse can be triggered through a myriad of approaches including imagnistic work, dream work, journal writing, body work, hypnosis, emotive work, and art therapy. In reference to art therapy, Fredrickson (1992) stated that it allowed for the re-creations of a portion of memory and served as a trigger of repressed memories. "Art therapy can be used as the major source of memory recovery or as an adjunct to other forms of recall" (p. 99). Roland (1993) found that visualization techniques and concrete construction may be effective in triggering blocked memories of abuse.

Guided imagery, flooding, drugs, and hypnosis may elicit unmanageable levels of intensify in some clients (Enns, et al., 1995). Hypnosis seems to be the most controversial of techniques since subjects vary in their level of suggestibility. Additionally, results of hypnosis have been unreliable (Myers, 1996). Each of these methods is accused of endorsing the possibility of sexual abuse where none exists. "Suggestion is an integral aspect of therapy, a central component to healing, and cannot be completely avoided (Yapko, 1994; Enns et al., 1995).

Even questioning a client about sexual abuse has met with criticism. Although some direct questions may be necessary, questions should be open-ended and allow the client to explore new areas. Memories may be influenced by questions (APA, 1994; Geoni, 1994). Enns and her colleagues (1995) recommended the following questions when working with a possible sexual abuse survivor (p. 236):

1. What do you remember?
2. What types of images did you see in your mind?
3. How did you feel then and now?
4. What were you thinking?
5. What types of recent experiences have triggered fear or other uncomfortable feelings?

Conscious memories of sexual abuse as well as "forgotten" memories should be considered accurate and valid (Enns et al., 1995). Retrieval of memories may modify the form of the memory and influence the conviction about the truth of the memory (APA, 1994; Geoni, 1994; Myers, 1994a). "Every time we recall an event, we must reconstruct memory, and with each recollection the memory may be changed-colored by succeeding events, other people's recollections or suggestions, increased understanding, or a new context" (Loftus, 1994, cited in Pendergrast, 1995, p. 104).

Recovery of memories associated with childhood sexual abuse has met with much criticism (Dawes, 1988; Loftus & Ketcham, 1991; Wakefield & Underwager, 1992; Loftus, 1993; Ofshe & Watters, 1993; Simonds, 1994; Stayton, 1994). The next section will focus on the retrieval of "nonexistent" memories of childhood sexual abuse.

FALSE MEMORY SYNDROME

In 1992, the False Memory Syndrome Foundation (FMSF) was formed in Philadelphia to promote education and public awareness of the damage of recovered memory therapy (Ofshe & Watters, 1994). False memory syndrome involves "a condition in which a person's identity and interpersonal relationships are centered around a memory of traumatic experience which is objectively false but in which the person strongly believes" (cited in Enns et al, 1995, p. 183). The FMSF criticizes recovered memory therapy:

> Unlike treatments intended to aid patients suffering from the shock of rape or grappling with lifelong memories of childhood sexual abuse, the axiom of recovered memory therapy is that the patient will have no knowledge of the sexual trauma before treatment. Patients can begin the therapy with no memories of abuse and finish with the belief that they suffered endless horrible molestations or rapes-often by their parents. (Ofshe & Watters, 1994, p. 1)

As Enns and her colleagues (1995) noted, the term "false memory syndrome" was created by the foundation for advocacy purposes; therefore, it does not represent a scientific endorsement, a point Spring (1996) supported. Additionally, Spring (1996) stressed that the FMSF bases their claims on research with normal memory, not traumatic memory (see Appendix I). On the other hand, the FMSF argues the following points (Pride, 1986; Gardner, 1992; Loftus, 1992; Ofshe & Watters, 1993; Wylie, 1993; Yapko, 1994):

1. therapists are intentionally or unintentionally planting false memories of sexual abuse through suggestion, pressure, and nontraditional methods such as hypnosis, body, dream, and art therapies;

2. therapists lack information about the nature of memories, viewing memories as exact copies of past events;

3. therapists mistakenly believe that amnesia for abuse is common;

4. therapists who specialize in abuse issues are poorly trained or are motivated by making money on the so called "child abuse industry"

5. therapists describe sexual abuse as the source of all a client's problems;

6. therapists encourage clients to pursue "frivolous" legal claims against parents;

7. self-help groups and books increase the likelihood that a client will develop false memories

Some individuals feel that the FMSF was created as a backlash against sexual abuse survivors (Myers, 1994b; Bloom, 1995; Enns et al., 1995; Gedney, 1995; Robbins, 1995). Specifically, some state that the FMSF emerged from a family vendetta against a woman who claimed that her patents sexually abused her (Freyd, 1993; Enns et al. 1995). Additionally, the FMSF appears focused on female survivors and their female therapists which reinforces the traditional stereotype of women as gullible and suggestible (Bass & Davis, 1994; Enns 1995).

> It is important to note that, those who make accusations based on "recovered memories" are not consciously lying, even if their version of the past may be incorrect. For them, the memories are real, sometimes even more compelling than memories of actual events from childhood. Given that, how can anybody argue that all, or at least most, of these "memories" are inaccurate? (Pendergrast, 1995, p. 86)

The validity of recovered memories has been questioned due to the lack of well-structured, research investigations as well as the complexity of memory recovery (Herman & Schatzow, 1987; Ernsdorff & Loftus 1993; Brenneis, 1994; Lindsay & Read, 1994). Therapists and researchers do not know how to gage the accuracy of memories based on true events from those based on false events (Geoni, 1994).

Therapist suggestions, level of hypnotizability, and group work may result in the development of false memories (Spray, 1994). "To distinguish between the Scylla of real sexual abuse and the Charybdis of so-called 'false or recovered memory' is a formable task, which confronts even the experienced analyst with complex theoretical and technical problems" (Ware, 1995, p. 18). Out of the previously mentioned methods, art therapy has received the least criticism as an approach to working with sexual abuse memories.

ART THERAPY AND MEMORIES

Art is a powerful mode that bridges memory, behavior, affect, sensation, and knowledge (Harding, 1973; Greenburg & van der Kolk, 1987; Braun, 1988; Hale, 1990; Jacobson, 1994). In addition, art may aid in the retrieval of forgotten memories, thereby providing a safe medium for exposing long-held secrets (Golub, 1985; Johnson, 1987; Bowers, 1992; Glaister, 1994; Simonds, 1994). Complicated or preverbal experiences can often be expressed through drawings (Edwards, 1986; Glaister, 1994).

> asking a child to draw a comparison of self young, self now, and a prior traumatic event, provide cognitive indicators regarding memory of the event, emotional indicators, and indictors of self-image. It is speculated that memories of the trauma are mediated by length of time since disclosure, psychological defenses, and introduction of therapy. (Burgess, 1988, p. 72)

The "painting cure" refers to the retrieval and integration of traumatic memories through art (van der Kolk, 1987). "When given the opportunity, the victim will project the memory of the traumatic experience, whether it is conscious or not, onto art medium by means of a symbolic language which results in a visual dialogue" (Spring, 1993, p. 1). The term visual dialogue was coined by Spring in 1978.

Some researchers agree that memories of traumatic events may be recorded in sensorimotor form (Schimek, 1975; Fredrickson, 1992). "It is likely, at times of overwhelming stimulation and terror in the moments of trauma, that the more highly developed cognitive system is bypassed and the event is recorded in photographic form, as a global record, unintegrated conceptually with other memories through normal associative links" (Johnson, 1987, p. 9). One argument centers on whether or not art represents an actual memory. Horovitz (1996) and Cohen (1996) felt that art work may represent actual memories for some clients. "It seems clear that Fredrickson, Davis, and others are willing not only to allow dreams, feelings, and artwork to be labeled memories, but to allow the content of those dreams and feelings to be labeled as accurate memory as well" (Ofshe & Watters, 1994, p. 85) My feelings about art as representing actual memories is mixed. Although I feel that art work can trigger memories of abuse, labeling as a memory is the responsibility of the client.

When a therapist tells a patient that her artwork, emotions, or physical symptoms are actually a type of memory of abuse, the presumption is strongly in the therapist's favor. The creation of this sort of abuse belief requires not coercion, complex influence, or thought-reform procedure. All that is necessary is that the client believe and trust the therapist. (Ofshe & Watters, 1994, p. 85)

While drawing pictures might access blocked feelings, is it wise to use those feelings to explore "the deeper nuances of suspicion and fear"? Where, we have to ask, will those nuances lead." If memories are triggered by a client's drawings or visual representations, the therapist has no reliable way of determining when these memories are accurate or inaccurate. Once again, caution is advised. (Loftus, 1995, p. 167)

Most of the research with memory retrieval and art therapy has focused on work with Dissociated Identity Disorder (DID). Much of the research cited in this text refers to DID clients as Multiple Personality Disordered (MPD) patients. Throughout the book, I use the terms as cited in the journal article, although it is recognized that MPD is no longer used as a diagnosis. Although not considered a personality disorder, DID clients are sometimes referred to as "Multiples."

The basic premise of using art therapy with this population is that memories of alter personalities can be confronted and incorporated. "Memory becomes fragmented as alters encapsulate knowledge, sensation, affect, and behaviors related to traumatic events in patients' life histories beginning in early childhood" (Kluft, 1993, p. 27). It appears that art therapy is an effective mode for integrating fractioned parts of self.

After a conference last year on the subject (ritual abuse), I started to use art therapy with clients. I asked people to draw at home on large paper with crayons and not to throw anything out. I asked them to draw a picture of themselves, but not to make it accurate. Sometimes I get fragments of the abuse scene. When people do drawings and show blood, it's not just virginal blood sometimes, but blood from cult abuse. (Pendergrast, 1995, p. 217)

Art helps to discover an MPD's past through graphic clues presented by alters at different stages of development (Jacobson, 1994). As alters emerge, other alters collaborate to defend or protect against the meaning of artwork. "An essentially nonverbal approach and metaphorical nature combined with an orientation to both process and product, make art therapy an important gateway for the retrieval and mastery of memory and affect" (Mills & Cohen, in Kluft, 1993, p. 39). Generally, the work of MPD's is characterized by movement, old trees, disintegration, tilt of 15 degrees or more, abstraction, and enclosure (Mills & Cohen, in Kluft, 1993). Old trees refer to branches falling apart from the trunks, chaotic branches, unrecognizable trees, and trees with trunks of minimal length.

Jacobson (1994) used art therapy with a patient suffering from MPD. As the therapeutic alliance progressed, the patient was able to connect with previously forgotten material. "Art may be therapeutically structured, however, which may circumvent the need for hypnosis to access traumatic memories" (p. 49). Jacobson concluded that art therapy was helpful in resynthesizing past experiences. Essentially, it helped to integrate dissociated material.

Many DID clients have experienced prior sexual abuse. Additional research on the effectiveness of art therapy in working with sexual abuse memories is needed.

> As therapists, we must be aware of the dark aspects of memory, being sensitive to a client's defenses against entering the dark cave alone or prematurely. For this, careful listening is needed, listening that supports and encourages without interpreting or judging the images and memories that come out from the dark cave within. Each client needs to find his or her own way. (Hale, 1990, p. 274)

Some of the following recommendations may be helpful when working with possible sexual abuse survivors.

1. establish guidelines for psychotherapy
2. help clients utilize self-help sources effectively
3. increase understanding of memory and its' fluidity
4. explore new ways to help clients dealing with memories of abuse
5. develop clients' cognitive skills so that they are able to deal with memories
6. establish informed consent with clients that outlines therapist's goals and practices
7. using preregistration interviews for sexual abuse survivor groups

Sexual abuse survivor groups have been criticized for giving rise to "false" memories of abuse. Horovitz (1996) noted the potential of group work to give rise to inaccurate memories. Although I have found that group work was effective when working with sexual abuse survivors, in that memories and feelings were integrated, I was cautious. I conducted preregistration interviews. Additionally, I required that people currently be in counseling for survivor issues. Generally, I based group membership on a similar level of previous counseling experiences. Given that art may sometimes trigger memories and strong affect, it was important to have a backup person, the client's therapist, to help process the material.

The nature of traumatic memory is still elusive. From the literature to date, art therapy appears to be a helpful method for dealing with traumatic childhood memories. This information has come primarily from working with DID clients who had also experienced sexual abuse. Research on using art therapy in dealing with sexual abuse memories is needed in order to further our understanding of this process.

REFERENCES

American Psychological Association: *Statement on memories of sexual abuse.* 1400 K Street, NW, Washington, DC, 20005: 202-682-2000, 1993.

American Psychological Association. *Diagnostic and statistical manual of mental disorders.*(4th ed.). Washington, DC, 1994.

Bass, E., & Davis, L.: *The courage to heal.* New York, Harper & Row, 1994.

Bloom, S.L.: When good people do bad things: Meditations on the Backlash." *The Journal of Psychohistory, 22(3)*: 280, 1995.

Blume, E.S.: *Secret survivors: Uncovering incest and its aftereffects in women.* New York, Ballantine, 1990.

Bowers, J.: Therapy through art: Facilitating treatment of sexual abuse. *Journal of Psychosocial Nursing and Mental Health Services, 30(6)*:15-23, 1992.

Braun, B.G.: The BASK model of dissociation. *Dissociation, 1,* 4-15, 1988.

Brenneis, C.B.: Belief and suggestions in the recovery of memories of childhood sexual abuse. *Journal of the American Psychoanalytic Association, 42(4)*: 1027 1053, 1994.

Briere, J.N.: *Child abuse trauma: Theory and treatment of the lasting effects.* Newbury Park, CA, Sage, 1992.

Briere, J., & Conte, J.: Self-reported amnesia for abuse in adults molested as children. *Journal of Traumatic Stress, 6*: 21-31, 1993.

Burgess, E.J.: Sexually abused children and their drawings. *Archives of Psychiatric Nursing, 2(2)*: 65-73, 1988.

Ceci, S.J., & Loftus, E.F.: "Memory work": A royal road to false memories? *Applied Cognitive Psychology, 8*: 351-364, 1994.

Chu, J.A., & Dill, D.L.: Dissociative symptoms in relations to childhood physical and sexual abuse. *American Journal of Psychiatry, 147(7)*: 887-892, 1990.

Cohen, F.: Personal communication from the former Chief of Art Psychotherapy at the Texas Research Institute of Mental Sciences, June 10, 1996.

Courtois, C.: *Healing the incest wound.* New York, Norton, 1988.

Davies, J.M., & Frawley, M.G.: *Treating the adult survivor of childhood sexual abuse: A psychoanalytic perspective.* New York, Basic Books, 1994.

Dawes, R.M.: Biases in retrospection. In: *Rational Choices in an Uncertain World.* San Diego, CA, Harcourt Brace Jovanovich, 1988.

Dewald, P.: Effects on an adult of incest in childhood: A case report. *Journal of American Psychoanalytic Association, 37*: 997-1114, 1989.

Edwards, B.: *Drawing on the artist within.* New York, Simon & Schuster, 1986.

Emerson, S.: Female student mental health counselors and child sexual abuse: Their's and their clients'. *Mental Health Counselor Education and Supervision, 28*: 15-20, 1988.

Enns C.Z., McNeilly, C.L., Corkery, J.M., & Gilbert, M.S.: The debate about delayed memories of child sexual abuse: A feminist perspective. *The Counseling Psychologist, 23(2)*: 181-279, 1995.

Ernsdorff, G.M., & Loftus, E.F.: Let sleeping memories lie? Words of caution about tolling the statue of limitation in cases of memory repression. *The Journal of Criminal Law & Criminology, 84(1)*: 129-174, 1993.

False Memory Syndrome Foundation: *False memory syndrome* brochure. Philadelphia, PA, 1992.

Fredrickson, R.: *Repressed memories: A journey to recovery from sexual abuse.* New York, Simon & Schuster, 1992.

Freud, S.: *Constructions in analysis,* S.E., 1937.

Freud, S.: *Repression.* In Strachey, T*he standard edition of the complete psychological works of Sigmund Freud, 14,* 1-66, 1957.

Freyd, J.: *Theoretical and personal perspectives on the delayed memory debate.* Paper presented at the Center for Mental Health at Foote Hospital's Continuing Education Conference. Ann Arbor, 1993.

Gardner, M.: True and false accusations of child sex abuse. Cresskill, NJ, Creative Therapeutics, 1992.

Gedney, N.: The backlash and beyond: The game of shame and blame. *The Journal of Psychohistory, 22(4)*:, 417, 439, 1995.

Geoni, T.: APA statement addresses the debate over "assisted" memory. *Skeptical Inquirer, 18*: 342-343, 1994.

Glaister, J.A.: Clara's story: Post-traumatic response and therapeutic art. *Perspectives in Psychiatric Care, 30(1)*: 17-22, 1994.

Golub, D.: Symbolic expression in post-traumatic stress disorder: Vietnam combat veterans in art therapy. *The Arts in Psychotherapy, 12*: 285-296, 1985.

Greenberg, M., & van der Kolk, B.: Retrieval and integration of traumatic memories with the "painting cure." In B. van der Kolk, *Psychological Trauma,* 1987.

Hale, S.E: Sitting on memory's lap. *The Arts in Psychotherapy, 17*: 269-274, 1990.

Harding, M.E.: *Psychic energy.* Princeton, NJ, Princeton University Press, 1973.

Herman, J., & Schatzow, E.: Recovery and verification of memories in childhood sexual trauma. *Psychoanalytic Psychology, 4*: 518-537, 1987.

Hewitt, S.K.: Preverbal sexual abuse: What two children report in later years. *Child Abuse & Neglect, 18(10)*: 821-826, 1994.

Horovitz, E.: Personal interview with the Director of Art Therapy at Hillside Children's Center, May 15, 1996.

Howard, B.: Art therapy as an isomorphic intervention in the treatment of a client with post-traumatic stress disorder. *The American Journal of Art Therapy, 28*: 79-86, 1989.

Jacobson, M.: Abreacting and assimilating traumatic, dissociated memories of MPD patients through art therapy. *Art Therapy: Journal of the American Art Therapy Association, 11(1)*: 48-52, 1994.

Johnson, D.: The role of the creative arts therapies in the diagnosis and treatment of psychological trauma. *Arts in Psychotherapy, 14*: 7-13, 1987.

Kihlstrom, J.F., & Hoyt, I.P.: Repression, dissociation, and hypnosis. In J.L. Singer, Repression and dissociation: *Implications for personality theory, psychopathology, and health.* Chicago, University of Chicago Press, 1990.

Kluft, E.S.: *Expressive and functional therapies in the treatment of multiple personality disorder.* Springfield, IL, Charles C Thomas, 1993.

Kuppersmith, J.: Discussion: Assessment and treatment of the unconscious sequelae of sexual abuse. *Psychological Psychoanalysis, 12*: 21, 1992.

Laidlaw, T.A., Malmo, C., & Associates: *Healing voices: Feminist approaches to therapy with women.* San Fransisco, Josey Bass, 1990.

Lindsay, D.S., & Read, J.D.: Incest resolution psychotherapy and memories of childhood sexual abuse: A cognitive perspective. *Applied Cognitive Psychology, 8*: 281-338, 1994.

Loftus, E.F.: Repressed memories of childhood trauma: Are they genuine? *Harvard Medical School Mental Health Letter, 9(9)*: 4-5, 1993.

Loftus, E., & Ketcham, K.: *The myth of repressed memory.* New York, St. Martin's Press, 1991.

Loftus, E.F., Polonsky, S., & Fullilove, M.T.: Memories of childhood sexual abuse: Remembering and repressing. *Psychology of Women Quarterly, 18*: 67-84, 1994.

Myers, D. G.: *Exploring psychology.* (3rd ed.). New York, Worth Publishers, 1996.

Myers, J.E. Adjudication of child sexual abuse cases. *The Future of Children, 4(2)*: 84-101, 1994.

Myers, J.E.: *The backlash.* Thousand Oaks, CA, Sage, 1994.

Ofshe, R., & Watters, E.: Making monsters. *Society*, 4-16, 1993.

Ofshe, R., & Watters, E.: *Making monsters: False memories, psychotherapy, and sexual hysteria.* New York, Charles Scribner's Sons, 1994.

Pendergrast, M.: *Victims of memory: Incest accusations and shattered lives.* Hinesburg, VT, Upper Access, Inc., 1995.

Pride, M.: *The child abuse industry: Outrageous facts about child abuse & everyday rebellions against a system that threatens every North American family.* Westchester, IL, Crossway Books, 1986.

Ratican, K.L.: Sexual abuse survivors: Identifying symptoms and special treatment considerations. *Journal of Counseling and Development, 71*:133-146, 1992.

Robbins, A.D.: False memories or hidden agendas? *The Journal of Psychohistory, 22(3)*: 305-311, 1995.

Roland, C.B.: Exploring childhood memories with adult survivors of sexual abuse: Concrete reconstruction and visualization techniques. *Journal of Mental Health Counseling, 15(4)*: 363-372, 1993.

Schimek, J.: A critical re-examination of Freud's concept of unconscious mental interpretation. *International Review of Psychoanalysis, 2*: 171-187, 1975.

Siegel, D., & Romig, C.: Treatment of adult survivors of childhood sexual assault: Imagery within a systemic framework. *The American Journal of Family Therapy, 16*: 229-241, 1988.

Simonds, S.L.: *Bridging the silence: Nonverbal modalities in the treatment of adult survivors of childhood sexual abuse.* New York, W.W. Norton, 1994.

Spray, K.J.: *Major concerns associated with recovered memories of childhood abuse. Information Analyses: ED 38,* 467, 1-14, 1994.

Spring, D.: *Shattered images: The phenomenological language of sexual trauma.* Chicago, IL, Magnolia Press, 1993.

Spring, D.: Personal communication with an art therapist in private practice, June 6, 1996.

Stayton, R.P.: Making meaner monsters: The polarization of the delayed/false memory controversy. *Journal of Child Sexual Abuse, 3(3)*: 127-134, 1994.

Terr, L.C.: *Unchained memories: True stories of traumatic memory loss.* New York, Basic Books, 1994.

van der Kolk, B.A.: *Psychological trauma.* Washington, DC, American Psychiatric Press, Inc., 1987.

van der Kolk, B., Biltz, R, & Burr, W.: Nightmares and trauma. *American Journal of Psychiatry, 141*: 187-190, 1984.

Wakefield, H., & Underwager, R.: Recovered memories of alleged sexual abuse: Lawsuits against parents. *Behavioral Science and the Law, 10*: 483-507, 1992.

Ware, R.C.: Scylla and charybdis: Sexual abuse or "false memory syndrome?" *Journal of Analytical Psychology, 40*: 5-22, 1995.

Williams, L.M.: Adult memories of childhood abuse: Preliminary findings from a longitudinal study. *The Advisor, 5*: 19-20, 1992.

Williams, L.M.: Recall of childhood trauma: A prospective study of women's memories of child sexual abuse. *Journal of Consulting and Clinical Psychology, 62(6)*: 1167-1176, 1994.

Wolf, E., & Alpert, J.: Psychoanalysis and sexual abuse: A review of the post-Freudian literature. *Psychoanalytic Psychology, 8*: 305-317, 1991.

Wylie, M.S.: Trauma and memory. *Family Therapy Networker, 17(5)*: 42-43, 1993.

Yapko, M.: Suggested guidelines for professional counselors. ACA *Guidepost,* September: 11, 1993.

Yapko, M.: *Suggestions of abuse: True and false memories of childhood sexual trauma.* New York, Simon & Schuster, 1994.

Zeig, J.K., (Ed): *Ericksonian Methods: The Essence of the Story.* New York, Brunner/Mazel Publishers, 1994.

Chapter 5

LEGAL ISSUES

P roving sexual abuse allegations can often be difficult, especially where delayed memories are concerned. Often, child abuse investigators seek physical evidence. If none is available, they resort to expert testimony and eyewitnesses. The next section will briefly describe factors involved in testifying as an expert witness in child abuse proceedings.

EXPERT TESTIMONY

According to Myers (1992), a common defense tactic is to attack professionals who interviewed the child. Improper interview techniques and leading questions may distort the child's memory or instill ideas of abuse even though it never occurred. The use of expert testimony is up to the courts. They decide whether or not evidence will assist the jury or help them to understand the evidence or to determine a fact in issue. Rule 702 of Federal Rules of Evidence states that:

> If scientific, technical, or other specialized knowledge will assist their trier of fact to understand the evidence or to determine a fact in issue, a witness qualified as an expert by knowledge, skills, experience, training, or education, may testify thereto in the form of an opinion or otherwise. (Myers, 1992, p. 240)

Lloyd (1990) expressed that expert testimony will be admitted only if the following four conditions have been met (p. 3):

1. the subject of the inference is so related to a special science, profession, business, or occupation that is beyond the knowledge of the average person OR (depending on the jurisdiction) even if the average person has some knowledge of the issues, the opinion would aid the jury.

2. the state of the art of the field permits a reasonable opinion to be given on the issues.

3. the witness is sufficiently skilled, knowledgeable and/or experienced in such a field to give a helpful opinion, and

4. the facts in evidence allow an opinion to be based upon them.

Myers (1992) reported that experts are questioned about educational attainments and degrees, specialization in a particular area of practice, and training in child sexual abuse. The extent of the person's experience with sexually-abused children will be scrutinized. Additionally, the expert should be thoroughly familiar with relevant professional literature. Myers (1992) asserted that membership in professional organizations, especially those focused on child abuse are essential. Publications on child sexual abuse will also be examined. It is particularly helpful if the person has been qualified as an expert on child abuse in prior court proceedings.

Expert testimony may be helpful in the following instances (Myers et al., 1989; Lloyd 1990): First, it can be used to determine if a child was sexually-abused based on the presence of behaviors observed in sexually-abused children, age inappropriate sexual knowledge, and consistency of symptoms and behaviors with sexual abuse survivors. Second, testimony can be used to determine a child's competence and credibility based on suggestibility and ability to distinguish between fact and fantasy. Third, a more limited purpose of testimony is for rehabilitating a child's credibility when there has been a delay in reporting abuse or inconsistent descriptions of abuse.

Expert testimony comes in the form of an opinion, a dissertation providing the jury with background information, or a response to a hypothetical question. Opinions should be based on reasonable certainty, consider of all the relevant facts, and demonstrate adequate understanding of pertinent clinical and scientific principles. The court will determine if the assumptions are reasonable, logical, and objective (Myers, 1992, 1993).

In civil proceedings, there is agreement that it is appropriate to give an opinion as to whether sexual abuse occurred (Myers et al., 1989; Lloyd, 1990). In criminal proceedings, experts cannot testify to the truthfulness of a child's statements; yet, they are able to provide information within which to interpret the child's testimony (Berliner & Barbiere, 1984).

Although art therapists can qualify as expert witnesses, they sometimes need to be backed up by psychiatrists or other professions (Levick et al., 1990; Wilkerson v. Pearson, 1985) before providing testimony.

> Art therapy is not a precise science. In the eyes of the law, it is not quantitative or experimentally verified. Thus, it remains for the art therapist involved in legal proceedings to prove that the probative value of the use of drawings outweighs the prejudicial effect. (Cohen-Liebman, 1995, p. 483)

Experts will be questioned as to the type of evaluation that was conducted, which serves as a basis for their clinical opinion. The next section will briefly consider the factors involved in sexual abuse evaluations.

EVALUATIONS

Evaluations of sexual abuse take one of two approaches. The first approach, the indicator approach, relies on the identification of discriminating elements of cases (Faller, 1984; Benedek & Schetsky, 1985; de Young, 1986; Green, 1986; Gardner 1987). Characteristics associated with true or false cases are the basis of forming the opinion (Berliner & Conte, 1993). As discussed in Chapter 3,

> There is no evidence of an indicator which is determinative of abuse. However, we also recognize that there are many patterns of indicators or case characteristics, some dealing with the child, some the allegation context, and others involving external variables which taken together may reliably influence the professional judgment or opinion about what happened. (Berliner & Conte, 1993, p. 122)

The indicator approach is controversial. One assessment based on indicators, the Sexual Abuse Legitimacy (SAL) Scale (Gardner, 1987) has met with criticism in court proceedings. In one case, it was used to convict a perpetrator. On appeal, the court found that the scale was not supported by validity evidence (Page v. Zordon, 1990). As a result, the court overturned the conviction.

The standards approach specifies the demeanor of the profession who conducts the sexual abuse evaluation. The American Academy of Child and Adolescent Psychiatry (AACAP) and American Professional Society on the Abuse of Children (APSAC) have outlined policies for practitioners. The guidelines for AACAP suggest that the use of children's drawings, videotaping, psychological testing of both parents, and medical exams are essential in providing evidence of sexual abuse (Berliner & Conte, 1993). Similarly, the APSAC provided guidelines regarding assessment aides such as drawings, dolls, and other psychological tools.

Disclosure of the sexual abuse is often marked by denial, especially when the child is insecure, frightened, or threatened (Lister, 1982; MacFarlane & Krebs, 1986; Courtois, 1988; Dziech & Schudson, 1989; Sorensen & Snow, 1991). When retrospectively analyzing 630 cases of alleged child sexual abuse, Sorensen and Snow (1991) found only 11 percent of the subjects disclosed the abuse during the initial interview. Also, 79 percent of the children denied their abuse or were tentative when disclosing it. "Policies and procedures geared only to those children in active disclosure not only fail to recognize the needs of the majority but may actually place children at increased risk" (p. 12). Hibbard and Hartman (1993) agreed that one interview or one interviewer is sometimes not sufficient in gathering evidence of sexual abuse.

ART THERAPY ASSESSMENTS IN COURT

The relevancy of artwork as evidence is considered mute by some. Horovitz (1996) submitted the artwork of a girl who was sexually-abused and the court did not consider it as relevant. Lloyd (1990) cited the technical definition of relevant evidence (p. 7):

> Relevant evidence means evidence having any tendency to make the existence of any fact that is of consequence to the determination of the action more probable or less probable than it would be without the evidence (Federal Rule of Evidence 401).

According to Cohen-Liebman (1995), drawings are acceptable methods for interviewing children suspected being sexually-abused. "Since the victim's own artwork is the visual documentation of the molestation, he or she can benefit from this recollective tool when accurate retrospection is required" (Landgarten, 1987, p. 33). Researchers agree that drawings provide valuable information about the abuse and therefore can serve as evidence (Burgess et al., 1981; Kelley, 1984 & 1985; Landgarten, 1987; Miller et al., 1987; Boat & Everson, 1988; Lyons, 1993; Steward et al., 1993). Additionally, art therapy is probably the least intimidating way to evaluate a child (Naitove, 1980; Stember, 1980; Kelley, 1984; Johnson, 1987; Manning, 1987; Sidun & Rosenthal, 1987; Goodwin, 1989; Malchiodi, 1990; Powell & Faherty, 1990; Cohen-Liebman, 1995).

At a National Symposium, Naitove (1985) found that professionals used the following tools more often when evaluating possible sexual abuse: art, movement, martial arts, drama, creative writing, music, and anatomically correct dolls. Human figure drawings, such as Draw A Person Test and the House-Tree-Person Test, are the more commonly used assessments. The Kinetic Family Drawing is also used in evaluating possible sexual abuse (Lyons, 1993; Cohen, 1996; Horovitz, 1996). If determination of sexual abuse relies heavily on diagnostic opinion and recommendations, these assessments are more vulnerable to cross-examination (Schetsky & Benedek, 1992; Lyons, 1993).

Being more direct than expert witnesses, drawings are useful because they review conflicts and unconscious perceptions of the victim (Cohen-Liebman, 1995). Kelley (1985) found that drawings of a 4-year-old girl were helpful in identifying the perpetrator, given that many people were suspected. Additionally, she asserted that drawings can be valuable in convincing adults when they doubt a child's story. As Kelley (1985), Cohen (1996) found that a young victim identified her perpetrator during a family session when the members were drawing the family. She was the only member who included an uncle, a frequent visitor to the home. He was later identified as the perpetrator.

Although most therapists agree that drawings can be considered evidence of sexual abuse, there is disagreement as to whether an art therapist can qualify as an expert witness. Spring (1996), Cohen (1996), and Horovitz (1996) have all served as expert witnesses with varying outcomes (see Appendix I). Cohen (1996) and Horovitz (1996) found that their profession was attacked. All three expressed frustration with the legal process. Cohen (1996) recently attended a seminar at the University of Houston which discussed the ability of art therapists to serve as expert witnesses. Essentially, only forensic psychologists or psychiatrists can be considered expert witnesses. Cohen (1996) provided a list of questions commonly asked of expert witnesses, which appears in Appendix II.

In the future, Cohen (1996) recommends that art therapists try to have a medical backup so that indicators of abuse can be validated. She felt that art therapists do not have to serve as expert witnesses; yet, they can have a healing effect when working with survivors. Horovitz (1996) suggests that if an art therapist does have to serve as an expert witness, he or she should watch how they word their descriptions. Also, she felt that it was beneficial to have supervision by a psychiatrist; therefore, the person would be less likely to be torn apart in court proceedings. Spring (1996) warns that practitioners should not jump to conclusions since most material in therapy is self-reported, not hard evidence. Also, she recommends using well-documented assessments and clinical notes. In a personal communication, Spring stated that licensed therapists who have an ATR-BC are often accepted as expert witnesses. It is the unlicensed ATR that has the most difficulty in the courtroom, particularly if they lack education and experience.

Additional information is needed on the use of drawings in court proceedings and the ability of art therapists to qualify as expert witnesses. This chapter presented some of the pertinent issues involved in legal proceedings. The next few chapters will discuss individual, group, and family art therapy with sexual abuse survivors. Research to date and case illustrations will be presented.

REFERENCES

Benedek, E.P., & Schetsky, D.H.: *Emerging issues in child psychiatry and the law.* New York, Brunner/Mazel, 1985.

Berliner, L., & Barbieri, M.K.: The testimony of the child victim of sexual assault. *Journal of Social Issues, 40(2)*: 125-137, 1984.

Berliner, L., & Conte, J.R.: Sexual abuse evaluations: Conceptual and empirical obstacles. *Child Abuse & Neglect, 17*: 111-125, 1993.

Boat, B.W., & Everson, M.D.: Interviewing young children with anatomical dolls. *Child Welfare, LXVII(4)*: 337-352, 1988.

Burgess, A.W., McCausland, M.P., & Wolbert, W.A.: Children's drawings as indicators of sexual trauma. *Perspectives in Psychiatric Care, 19(2)*: 50-57, 1981.

Cohen, F.: Personal communication from the former Chief of Art Psychotherapy at the Texas Research Institute of Mental Sciences, June 10, 1996.

Cohen-Liebman, M.S.: Drawings as judiciary aids in child sexual abuse litigation: A compost list of indicators. *The Arts in Psychotherapy, 22(5)*: 475-483, 1995.

Courtois, C.: *Healing the incest wound.* New York, W. W. Norton, 1988.

de Young, M.: A conceptual model for judging the truthfulness of a young child's allegations of sexual abuse. *American Journal of Orthopsychiatry, 56*: 550-559, 1986.

Dziech, B., & Schudson, C.: *On trial.* Boston, MA, Beacons Press, 1989.

Faller, K.C.: Is the child victim of sexual abuse telling the truth? *Child Abuse & Neglect, 8*: 473-481, 1984.

Gardner, R.A.: *The parental alienation syndrome and the differentiation between fabricated and genuine child sex abuse.* Cresskill, NJ, Creative Therapeutics, 1987.

Goodwin, J.: *Sexual abuse.* Chicago, Year Book Medical, 1989.

Green, A.H.: True and false allegations of sexual abuse in child custody disputes. *Journal of the American Academy of Child Psychiatry, 25*: 449-456, 1986.

Hibbard, R.A., & Hartman, G.L.: Components of child and parent interview in cases of alleged sexual abuse. *Child Abuse & Neglect, 17*: 495-500, 1993.

Horovitz, E.: Personal interview with the Director of Art Therapy at Hillside Children's Center, May 15, 1996.

Johnson, D.R.: The role of the creative arts therapies in the diagnosis and treatment of psychological trauma. *The Arts in Psychotherapy, 14*: 7-13, 1987.

Kelley, S.J.: The use of art therapy with sexually-abused children. *Journal of Psychosocial Nursing, 22(12)*: 12-18, 1984.

Kelley, S.J.: Drawings: Critical communications for sexually-abused children. *Pediatric Nursing, 11*: 1985.

Landgarten, H.: *Family art psychotherapy.* New York, Brunner/Mazel, 1987.

Levick, M.F., Safran, D.S., & Levine, A.J: Art therapist as expert witnesses. A Judge delivers a precedent-setting decision. *The Arts in Psychotherapy, 17:* 49-53, 1990.

Lister, E.: Forced silence: Neglected dimensions of trauma. *American Journal of Psychiatry, 139(7)*: 872-876, 1982.

Lloyd, D.W.: *Mental health professions as expert witnesses in child sexual abuse cases: A legal perspective on the controversies.* Paper presented at the 98th American Psychological Association Convention. Boston, MA, APA, 1-23, 1990.

Lyons, S.J.: Art psychotherapy evaluations of children in custody disputes. *The Arts in Psychotherapy, 20:* 153-159, 1993.

MacFarlane, K., & Krebs, S.: Techniques for interviewing and evidence gathering. In MacFarlane & Waterman, *Sexual abuse of young children.* New York, Gulliford, 1986.

Malchiodi, C.A.: *Breaking the silence: Art therapy with children from violent homes.* New York, Brunner/Mazel, 1990.

Manning, T.M. Aggression depicted in abused children's drawings. *Arts in Psychotherapy, 14*: 15-24, 1987.

Myers, J.B., Bays, J., Becker, J., Berliner, L., Corwin, D.L., & Saywitz, K.J.: Expert testimony in child sexual abuse litigation. *Nebraska Law Review, 68*: 1-145, 1989.

Miller, T.W., Veltkamp, L.J., & Janson, D.: Projective measures in the clinical evaluation of sexually-abused children. *Child Psychiatry and Human Development, 18(1)*: 47-57, 1987.

Myers, J.E.: *Evidence in child abuse and neglect* (2nd Ed. Vol.1). New York, John Wiley & Sons, 1992.

Myers, J.E.: Expert testimony regarding child sexual abuse. *Child Abuse & Neglect, 17:* 175-183, 1993.

Naitove, C.E.: Arts therapy with sexually-abused children. In S. M. Sgroi, *Handbook of clinical intervention in child sexual abuse*. Boston, MA, Lexington Books, 1980.

Naitove, C.E.: Protecting our children: The fight against molestation. *The Arts in Psychotherapy, 12*: 115-116, 1985.

Page v. Zordon, 564 So. 2d 500 (FL: App 2 Dist., 1990).

Powell, L. &Faherty, S.L. Treating sexually-abused latency age girls. *The Arts in Psychotherapy, 17:* 35-47, 1990.

Schetsky, D.H., & Benedeck, E.P.: *Clinical handbook of child psychiatry and the law.* Baltimore,MD, Williams & Wilkins, 1992.

Sidun, N.M., & Rosenthal, R.H.: Graphic indicators of sexual abuse in draw-a-person tests of psychiatrically hospitalized adolescents. *The Arts in Psychotherapy, 14:* 25-33, 1987.

Sorenson, T., & Snow, B.: How children tell: The process of disclosure in child sexual abuse. *Child Welfare, LXX(1):* 3-15, 1991.

Spring, D.: Personal communication with an art therapist in private practice, June 6, 1996.

Stember, C.J.: Art therapy: A new use in the diagnosis and treatment of sexually-abused children. In U.S. Department of Health and Human Services, Sexual Abuse of Children Selected Readings (pp 59-63). Washington, DC, U.S. Government Printing Office, 1980.

Steward, M.S., Bussey, K., Goodman, G.S., & Saywitz, K.J.: Implications of developmental research for interviewing children. *Child Abuse & Neglect, 17:* 25-37, 1993.

Wilkerson v. Pearson, 210 N.J. Super. 333 (Ch. Div., 1985).

Chapter 6

CASE WORK UTILIZING ART THERAPY

PROFILE OF SEXUAL ABUSE SURVIVORS

Sexual abuse survivors suffer from a variety of somatic and emotional complaints. Recurrent headaches were very frequently reported: "These headaches are not only a physical manifestation of repressed rage and anxiety but are also a form of self punishment" (Herman, 1981, p. 108). Herman (1981) explained that depression was the most typical expression of sexual abuse conflicts, which may also be related to repressed anger. Posttraumatic stress disorder was another common expression of childhood sexual abuse (Lindberg & Distad, 1985; Greenwald & Leitenburg, 1990; Peacock, 1991; Rowan & Foy, 1993; Glaister, 1994; Rowan et al., 1994; Enns et al., 1995). Additionally, survivors reported having feelings of being stigmatized and isolated (Gomez-Schwartz et al., 1990).

> Consumed with inner rage, they nevertheless rarely caused trouble to anyone but themselves. In their own flesh, they bore the repeated punishment for crimes committed against them in childhood. (Herman, 1981, p. 108)

Characterized by selflessness, sexually-abused females experience somatic problems, emotional constriction, low self-image, and internalized guilt and blame (Mayer, 1983). Since these women did not learn to protect themselves, the cycle of abuse often continued into adulthood when they entered into relationships with abusive men (Herman, 1981). This was evident from some of the case examples that will be discussed.

> Thus did the victims of incest grow up to become archetypally feminine women: sexy without enjoying sex, repeatedly victimized yet repeatedly seeking to lose themselves in the love of an overpowering man, contemptuous of themselves and of other women, hard-working, giving, and self-sacrificing. (Herman, 1981, p. 108)

Mayer (1983) observed that female sexual abuse survivors had difficulty dealing with other women. For instance, abused women often feel estranged from their mother: "It is a complicated relationship, full of guilt, anger, distance, loneliness, and feelings of deep betrayal" (Kosof, 1985, p. 17). The difficulty experienced in the mother-daughter relationship seemed to generalize to relationships with other women. In addition, Kosof (1985) discovered that female survivors turn their problems inward, resulting in problems with sexual identity and substance abuse: Often, sexual abuse survivors became prostitutes, drug addicts, nuns, asexual, or homosexual.

Hunter (1990) found that sexually-abused boys were more likely to be physically injured than girls. As with female survivors, males had a paradoxical view of their bodies: "They view them as misshapen, ugly or disgusting, yet possessing some power or ability that causes people to be driven to be sexual with them" (Hunter, 1990, p. 60). Male survivors had problems with relationships, were depressed, and engaged in substance abuse (Krug, 1989).

Disassociation, blocked affect, and self-blame were universal characteristics of abused males (Mayer, 1983). Since men are socialized in our culture to initiate sexual contact, the internalization of blame can be quite extreme. Yet, "the abuse has nothing to do with his behavior, he was merely the most convenient target; he is powerless" (Hunter, 1990, p. 71). Since there is a tendency in society and particularly among sexual abuse investigators to see the male as a willing participant, he is less likely to be viewed as a victim; therefore, he will blame himself for the abuse.

Both male and female survivors learn to distrust their view of reality since "covert contact is particularly powerful in teaching the victimized person not to trust his thoughts and perceptions of the world" (Hunter, 1990, p. 64). Oppression appears to be the basis of sexual abuse:

> One of the gravest obstacles to the achievement of liberation is that oppressive reality absorbs those within it and thereby acts to submerge men's consciousness. Functionally, oppression is domesticating. (Freire, 971, p. 36)

Disassociation, denial, and repression were common defense mechanisms used to cope with the abusive situation. From these profiles, we can see how guilt and shame were strong factors in the silence that surrounded sexual abuse. "The sexually-abused child's [person's] experience is based upon invasion of every kind of boundary: Upon love which is partly felt as hatred and pain; upon secrecy, which is bound up in lies; upon dishonesty with oneself and to others, and in creating false impressions and presenting false appearances" (Sagar in Case & Dalley, 1990, p. 113). Because the child or adolescent was not in a position of power, the responsibility for the abuse became internalized, resulting in a variety of emotional and somatic symptoms; therefore, treatment issues with sexually-abused people should focus on the following: trust, anger, body image, and relationships issues (Malchiodi, 1990).

CASE WORK WITH SEXUAL ABUSE SURVIVORS

Art therapy with sexual abuse survivors may occur for the purpose of diagnostic assessment or for treatment of sexual abuse issues. In general, art therapy is helpful in assisting people, particularly children, in giving voice to their traumatic experience (Coulson et al., 1994). Sgroi (1982) suggested the following goals and objectives when using art therapy with sexually-abused individuals (p. 277):

1. Introduce client to creative expression and provide gratifying arts experiences; integrate ego and enhance self-esteem.
2. Elicit verbal and nonverbal statements of internalized conflict; separate self from trauma.
3. Develop alliance with the therapist to reaffirm client strengths.
4. Accelerate maturation of delayed cognitive and functional behavior patterns to age appropriate level.

A skilled art therapist can furnish unparalleled information regarding sexual abuse, particularly with young victims or with severely traumatized or non verbal children. "For adult survivors of childhood sexual abuse, the nonverbal modalities of art and movement can serve as a bridge between the unspoken and the spoken, between the unknown and the known, between the unconscious and the conscious" (Simonds, 1994).

As discussed previously, sexual abuse survivors often have difficulty dealing with their emotions. "Using play and art materials, because of the tactile, physical nature which relates directly to sensation and emotional feelings, is arguably the most useful therapy for children [adults] who have been sexually-abused" (Sagar in Case

& Dalley, 1990, p. 113). Art therapy may be helpful in answering the following questions (Burgess & Holmstrom, 1979, p. 294):

1. Is the sexually traumatized person in an acute phase of disorganization?

2. Is the person fixated at the point of trauma either by:
   a. showing repetition of the trauma image or
   b. showing chronic disorganization?

3. Has the person missed experiencing or mastering developmental tasks due to the sexual trauma continuing over an extended time period?

4. Are their any indicators of the person's integrating the trauma as a life experience?

Art therapy with sexual abuse survivors has the potential of revealing client strengths as well as weaknesses. Additionally, it can stimulate affect. Since splitting off of emotion is a characteristic response to sexual abuse, art can offer an opportunity for integration. This fact will be evident in some of the following case examples. Please note that I have used diagnostic terms that the author has cited in his/her writing. It is recognized that Posttraumatic Stress Disorder (PTSD) and Dissociative Identity Disorder (DID) are more current classifications than the terms used by some of the following authors.

ART THERAPY WITH CHILD SURVIVORS

Anger associated with the sexual abuse can be a powerful emotion, one which our culture teaches women and children not to express openly:

> When emotionally disturbed children experience strong emotional feelings, it is often hard for them to identify their feelings and their source. Often these children see themselves much as they see the monster, ie. "mean, bad, scary, and unloved"; the child is the monster. (Volgi-Phelps, 1985, p. 35)

Volgi-Phelps (1985) employed art therapy with emotionally-disturbed children in order to help them "let their monsters out." Using the case approach, she discovered that the monsters started to appear when the children were comfortable with the art materials and the therapist. Volgi-Phelps described these monsters (mangy animals or grotesque figures with weapons) as symbols for anger, hate, loneliness, sadness, and guilt. Through art, the child learned to manage emotion, promote self-concept, and learn socially acceptable ways for expressing feelings (Volgi-Phelps, 1985).

Kelley (1984) conducted an exploratory study using art therapy with ten sexually-abused children. She compiled the work of three males and seven females (3 - 10 years of age) who were receiving victim counseling at a large urban teaching hospital. During their individual sessions, the subjects were asked to draw a self-portrait, a picture of the offender, a drawing of "what happened," and a picture of a "whole person." Fifty percent of the children drew self-portraits that were tiny, possibly revealing low self-esteem. Thirty percent omitted their hands in the self-portrait which may reveal helplessness. Twenty percent drew figures with questionable gender identity. Only 50 percent of the children would draw their offender. Some children were able to verbalize anger toward the perpetrator. One child gave the perpetrator a black eye. Other children drew themselves next to the perpetrator. Fifty percent of the children were able to draw "what happened." "Children who were previously reluctant to discuss the assaults became more verbal and more willing to share their thoughts and feelings surrounding the sexual abuse" (Kelley, 1984, p. 17). The author reported that the drawings were used as evidence in court.

Three sisters from a family with a history of sexual abuse participated in art therapy (Dufrene, 1994). The girls were sexually-abused by their grandfather and stepfather and physically abused by their father. Anne (7), Andrea (8), and Nancy (9) were treated together. Ambiguous sexuality, long eyelashes, omission of facial features, wedge shapes, sexualized features, and heart images surfaced in their artwork. Dufrene (1994) felt that the children were able to process their feelings about sexual abuse and the perpetrator. Additionally, art therapy served as a teaching tool to prevent future abuse.

Stember (1978) treated a sexually-abused, 11-year-old girl through art therapy. Celia was a product of an interracial marriage and came from a severely abusive and neglectful home. She presented multiple problems such as aggressive behavior, minimal ego strength, and poor problem solving skills. Initially, Celia's artwork was stereotyped and defended. It depicted her low self-worth and hostility. Progressively, she learned to express her feelings through art and became more confident in her abilities. Her death fantasies were replaced by empowering, positive survival statements. Toward the end of her therapy, Stember (1978) found that Celia was using art as a method for trying out new situations. "Her ability to relearn living skills indicates a high level of retrievability and growth. Art therapy played a crucial role in the redirecting of an activated drive state" (Stember, 1978, p.109).

Briggs and Lehmann (1989) utilized art therapy with a four year old female. When visiting a family friend, the little girl went in to the house to use the toilet and was sexually-abused by an elderly man. Armless figures, floating images, and bathroom scenes predominated her artwork. Through art therapy treatment, she gradually began to master the trauma. For example, her later figures had arms revealing empowerment.

Peake (1987) used art therapy with a severely sexually and physically abused boy. David was a seven-year-old, Caucasian male who had two older brothers. His father perpetrated sexual tortures on all the children, partially castrating one of David's brothers in front of him. David's father was classified as a paranoid schizophrenic. The mother was severely physically abused by the father and did not report any of the incidents. After his mother's hospitalization for depression and his father's incarceration, David was placed in foster care. In the first year of therapy, Peake (1987) reported that David's artwork had a destructive pattern yet vacillated between violence and hope for peace.

> Used as a dominant defense mechanisms in children who have suffered from severe abuse and trauma, the "badness" which the children interject as result of abuse is projected onto others as all good or all bad, thus interfering with the children's ability to realistically assess the behavior of others or the effects of their own behavior on others. (Peake, 1987, p. 42-43)

David's tree drawing was characterized as an inverted, castrated phallus. The tree also lacked a branch system, limiting one's contact with the environment (Buck, 1987; Peake, 1987). David's drawing of Superman was wedge shaped and lacked hands. Additionally, his cape was transparent, a characteristic often noted in the work of sexual abuse survivors (Malchiodi, 1990). A frequent image that David used was a rainbow. David described the rainbow as a sign from God that "He wouldn't do something bad again." Peake (1987) interpreted the rainbow as meaning "God the father, initially portrayed as cruel and punitive and matching prominent traits of David's natural father, later promises never to be destructive again in the same manner"

(p. 46). Phallic themes and images of castration continued to surface in his art. Through art therapy, Peake (1987) expressed that David was better able to deal with his own weaknesses and improve his relationships with others. "The bright, traumatized children, however, through the mechanisms of myth or allegory seem to choose or invent a storyline that symbolically contains parallels to the events that occurred in their own painful past" (Peake, 1987, p. 57).

Myers-Garrett (1987) examined the role of contours in symbol formation with Billy, a nine-year-old, sexually-abused boy. She found that old symbols were detached and replaced by a new system of symbols:

> Through this process, a bridging between what happened in the past to children such as Billy and the present creates an organized internal structure with symbol formation that allows them to find a more congruent life space. (Myers,-Garrett, 1987, p. 45)

Her description of contours, avowed as essential to the therapeutic relationship, referred to field dependence and figure ground. "Where one ultimately wishes to make the unconscious conscious, the development of contours makes new perceptions possible" (Myers-Garrett, 1987, p. 46). Billy and his older brother were sexually violated by the husband of a babysitter. Billy was classified as mildly emotionally disturbed and was institutionalized. Collage work with Billy revealed symbols of power and aggression. Again, the theme of the superhero emerged. Billy's memory and fear of the abusive incident was integrated in a framework that could be dealt with effectively. As a result, he was empowered. Myers-Garrett (1987) stressed that this type of therapy is appropriate only for those individuals who had previous art therapy treatment.

Silvercloud (1983) worked with Joey, a six-year-old boy who was repeatedly sodomized by neighborhood boys. Stabbing motions, destructive themes, encapsulation, and cars were images in his work. Initially in his drawings, Joey represented himself as helpless and his perpetrators as powerful. Slowly, the roles were reversed. As Joey began to express his anger towards his perpetrators, his images of himself were gradually empowered.

ART THERAPY WITH ADULT SURVIVORS

Simonds (1992) found that expressive therapy was helpful in dealing with body image issues of a 19-year-old, female sexual abuse survivor. Janine suffered from anorexia, later bulimia, and depression. Asexual images appeared in her human figure drawings. As therapy progressed, Janine began to view herself as a curvy, feminine figure through a multimodal approach that combined art, music, and movement therapies.

Yates and Pawley (1987) used imaging when helping Martha, an adult, sexual abuse survivor, resolve her childhood trauma. Martha's mother died when she was 3-years-old. At the age of 4, her brother began sexually abusing her until she was 13 years old. Her sexual abuse appeared to interfere with her memories of her mother. Martha used complimentary colors, such as orange and blue, to color her work. Angry hands, floating eyes, phallic shapes, black hearts, and sharp kitchen utensils were some of the images that appeared in her work. Through art therapy, Martha was gradually able to recall her memories of her mother. She explored new methods of control and was able to freely express her affect.

Nez (1991) examined the archetypal images in the treatment of Vera, a 38-year-old, suspected sexual abuse survivor. Although Vera knew that she was physically and emotionally abused by her father, she had no distinct memories of sexual abuse; yet, she continually experienced anger towards her father and periods of depression. "As therapist, I became a collaborator in the rewriting of Vera's story, working with her to uncover the deeper significance of her imagery, and a comprehension of its underlying archetypal themes" (Nez, 1991, p. 123). Downing (1981) felt that discovering theses archetypal, mythical symbols helped the client to enhance self-understanding. Labyrinth shapes and mazes appeared in her first drawing. My work with an 8-year-old boy suspected of sexual abuse also revealed several mazes. Some therapists find that using maps or mazes are helpful in working with sexual abuse survivors: " Finding some sense of herself and her own boundaries seemed to be the function of the map, as well as expressing her anxiety about invasion of those boundaries and what may have been put inside her" (Sagar in Case & Dalley, 1990, p. 92-93). Clay work with Vera revealed images of caverns, a pregnant goddess, and old women. Religious associations were made to her clay pieces. As a result of archetypal art therapy, Vera's confidence improved and produced a transformation of limiting attitudes.

Using hypnoanalytic art therapy, Lemmon (1984) treated a 50-year-old Caucasian female. All artwork was done under hypnosis: the client was asked to draw the scene perceived during the age regression. Jean was physically and psychologically abused by both parents. Additionally, she was sexually-abused at the age of two by her father. The abuse continued for several years. As with David in the previous case example, Jean drew rainbows:

> The rainbow is a drawing done by those in a frame of mind representing change. Basically it is optimistic but still may show problems to be cleared. (Lemmon, 1994, p. 106)

Circles, hearts, and phallic trees were other images that appeared in Jean's work. Lemmon (1984) concluded that hypnoanalytic art therapy, while not appropriate for everyone, was best suited for highly resistant individuals.

Glaister (1994) used art therapy as treatment for posttraumatic response (PTR). She noted that PTR was observed in adults who experienced childhood sexual abuse. "After years of secrecy, fear, denial, repression, suppression, and/or maladaptive coping patterns, recovery for chronic survivors can be lengthy, painful, and arduous" (Glaister, 1994, p. 17). Glaister treated Clara, a 36 year old female suffering from PTR. For Clara, sexual abuse memories began early in life with several familial perpetrators. Her mother died when Clara was young and her father was alcoholic. Clara was the youngest of four children. At 16, Clara married an alcoholic and abusive husband. Four years later, he forced her to leave home and obtained custody of their two children. Clara remarried shortly after the divorce and remained with her second husband for 19 years. When she entered therapy, Clara reported feeling depressed, anxious, amnesic, and angry. In response to a smiling portrait with heavy black clouds above, Clara reported:

> There are two sides to me: One appears happy and smiling, but is really covering up the guilt, shame, fear, and pain. The other side is covered by dark clouds. These clouds are the dark secrets that need to come out. As long as the clouds are there, I still believe the put-downs: I'm no good; I can't do anything; I'm stupid; I'm crazy; I'm a misfit. (Glaister, 1994, p. 19)

Her tree drawing revealed a need for nurturance (fruit) and instability (shallow root system). Nine months into therapy, she drew herself as a tiny figure carrying a large weight on her head. Five months later, she drew a figure with no arms or feet. Clara's therapy continued for two and a half years. Glaister (1994) reported that "drawings at regularly spaced intervals provide a visual measurement of progress and change, from which clients can gain a sense of accomplishment and empowerment" (p. 22). Also, art therapy provided an opportunity to teach about the dynamics of abuse, relationships, patterns, and adaptive functioning.

Howard (1989) used art therapy as an isomorphic intervention with a woman suffering from Posttraumatic Stress Disorder (PTSD). Isomorphism was defined as a match of the style of therapeutic intervention to the style of problematic patterns manifested in PTSD; both involved imagery and distancing processes (Howard, 1989). Rachel was a 36-year-old, sexual abuse survivor hospitalized for sleep disturbance, suicidal thoughts, fatigue, and poor appetite. Work on nightmares began to trigger sexual abuse memories. Rachel was physically abused by her mother at an early age and sexually-abused by her father. She had a sister who was ten years younger. When she was 18, Rachel walked in after her father finished sexually abusing the younger sister. Rachel has been married twice with one child from her first marriage. Her first marriage was verbally and physically abusive. In art therapy, Rachel dealt with the traumatic images of her sexual abuse. She would often reexperience the affect associated with the abuse. Gradually, she began to problem solve through art. Using Beck's Depression Inventory as a pre and posttreatment measure, Howard (1989) found that Rachel displayed a significant reduction in stress and increased self-awareness.

Peacock (1991) introduced art therapy in the treatment of a 40-year-old, Caucasian woman suffering from Post Sexual Abuse Trauma (PSAT). Three standardized measures were used to assess changes in self-esteem, anxiety, and depression. Jane was hospitalized for depression and suicidal ideation. Jane's father was a prominent businessman who was alcoholic and severely abusive to the family. Jane had memory gaps until the age of 10. At the time of therapy, Jane was married with two adolescent sons. She was given daily art therapy sessions for the remaining 10 days of her hospitalization specifically for the purpose of recovering repressed memories, realizing affect, and increasing self-esteem. A nightmare of being raped produced an image of a person being crucified. Circles, encapsulated figures, figures lacking torsos, and tiny figures were just a few of the images that emerged. Peacock (1991) felt that art allowed Jane to create new responses in relation to her feelings about childhood. Additionally, drawings were related to actual memories. "Through art experiences, the client addressed intrusive imagery, released repressed affect related to childhood trauma, reframed and integrated abreacted material, and achieved increased self-awareness and control" (Peacock, 1991, p. 100). Her level of depression did not change.

Art therapy has also been used in the treatment of sexual abuse survivors suffering from Multiple Personality Disorder (MPD). Shapiro (1988) engaged in art therapy with Anne, a 23-year-old woman classified as MPD since the age of 15 years. At 3 years of age, Anne's father was sexually abusing her. Using shades of red, orange, and black, Shapiro (1988) reported that Anne's work was vaginal, violated, and bloody. Circles, floating images, and red doors also appeared in her work. Shapiro (1988) concluded that art therapy allowed Anne to bridge her inner and outer worlds.

Much of the information obtained on art therapy has been derived from case studies (Howard & Jakab, 1968; Stember, 1978; Goodwin, 1982; Kelley, 1984; Briggs & Lehmann, 1985; Spring, 1985; Volgi-Phelps, 1985; Levinson, 1986; Mackay, Gold & Gold, 1987; Rubin, 1987). Although this information provides insight on the use of art therapy, the case method has several limitations. First, case studies may not generalize to the larger population of survivors. Additionally, the observers are not blind and therefore may not be objective. Last, the case method does not utilize a comparison group. Despite these limitations, the case method has yielded valuable information on the use of art therapy with sexual abuse survivors. The case method provides the foundation for individuals to conduct research in the field. The next chapter will present an art therapy diagnostic assessment of an eight-year-old male suspected of being sexually-abused.

REFERENCES

Briggs, F., & Lehmann, K.: Significance of children's drawings in cases of sexual abuse. *Early Child Development and Care, 47*: 131-147, 1989.

Buck, J.N.: *The House-Tree-Person technique: Revised manual.* Los Angeles, Western Psychological Services, 1987.

Burgess, A.W., & Holmstrom, L.L.: *Rape: Crisis and recovery.* Bowie, Maryland, Robert J. Brady Co, 1979.

Case, C., & Dalley, T.: *Working with children in art therapy.* New York, Travistock/Routledge, 1990.

Coulson, K.W., Wallis, S., & Clark, H.: The diversified team approach in the treatment of incest families. *Psychotherapy in Private Practice, 13(2):* 19-43.

Downing, C.: *The goddess.* New York, Crossroad Publishing, 1981.

Dufrene, P.: Art therapy and the sexually-abused child. *Art Education, November:* 6-11, 1994.

Enns, C.Z., McNeilly, C.L., Corkery, J.M., & Gilbert, M.S.: The debate about delayed memories of child sexual abuse: A feminist perspective. *The Counseling Psychologist, 23(2)*: 181-279, 1995.

Freire, P.: *Pedagogy of the oppressed.* New York, Herder and Herder, 1971.

Glaister, J.A.: Clara's story: Post-traumatic response and therapeutic art. *Perspectives in Psychiatric Care, 30(1)*: 17-22, 1994.

Gomez-Schwartz, B., Horowitz, J. M., & Cardarelli, A. P.: *Child sexual abuse: Initial effects.* Newbury Park,CA, Sage, 1990.

Goodwin, J.: Use of drawings in evaluating children who may be incest victims. *Children and Youth Services Review, 4*: 269-278, 1982.

Greenwald, E., & Leitenberg, H: Post-traumatic stress disorder in a non-clinical and nonstudent sample of adult women sexually-abused as children. *Journal of Interpersonal Violence, 5*: 217-228, 1990.

Herman, J. L.: *Father-daughter incest.* Cambridge, MA, Harvard University Press, 1981.

Howard, B.: Art therapy as an isomorphic intervention in the treatment of a client with post-traumatic stress disorder. *The American Journal of Art Therapy, 28:* 79-86, 1989.

Howard, M.C. & Jakab, I.: Case studies of molested children and their art products. *Art Interpretation and Art Therapy, 2*: 72-89, 1968.

Hunter, M.: *Abused boys: The neglected victims of incest.* Lexington, MA, Lexington Books, 1990.

Kelley, S.J.: The use of art therapy with sexually-abused children. *Journal of Psychosocial Nursing, 22*: 12-18, 1984.

Kosof, A.: *Incest: Families in crisis.* New York, Franklin Watts, 1985.

Krug, R. S.: Adult male report of childhood sexual abuse by mothers: Case descriptors, motivations and long-term consequences. *Child Abuse & Neglect, 13:* 111-119, 1989.

Lemmon, K.W.: Hypnoanalytic art therapy with victims of rape and incest. *Medical*

Hypnoanalysis, July: 104-108, 1984.

Levinson, P.: Identification of child abuse in art and play products. *Art Therapy, 3(2)*: 61-66, 1986.

Lindberg, F.H., & Distad, L.J.: Post-traumatic stress disorders in women who experienced childhood incest. *Child Abuse and Neglect: The International Journal, 9:* 329-334, 1985.

Mackay, B., Gold, M., & Gold, E.: A pilot study in drama therapy with adolescent girls who have been sexually-abused. *The Arts in Psychotherapy, 14*: 77-84, 1987.

Malchiodi, C.A.: *Breaking the silence: Art therapy with children from violent homes.* New York, Brunner/Mazel, 1990.

Mayer, A.: *Incest: A treatment manual for therapy with victims, spouses, and offenders.* Holmes Beach, FL, Learning Publications, Inc, 1983.

Myers-Garrett, E.A.: The role of contours in symbol building with a victim of sexual abuse. *Pratt Institute Creative Arts Therapy Review, 8:* 45-51, 1987.

Nez, D.: Persephone's return: Archetypal art therapy and the treatment of a survivor of abuse. *The Arts in Psychotherapy, 18(2):* 123-130, 1991.

Peacock, M.E.: A personal construct approach to art therapy in the treatment of post sexual abuse trauma. *The American Journal of Art Therapy, 29*: 100-109, 1991.

Peake, B.: A child's odyssey toward wholeness through art therapy. *The Arts in Psychotherapy, 14*: 41-58, 1987.

Rowan, A.B., & Foy, D.W.: Posttraumatic stress disorder in child sexual abuse survivors. A literature review. *Journal of Traumatic Stress, 6*: 159-177, 1993.

Rowan, A.,B., Foy, D.W., Rodriguez, N., & Ryan, S.: Posttraumatic stress disorder in a clinical sample of adults sexually-abused as children. *Child Abuse and Neglect: The International Journal, 18*: 51-61, 1994.

Rubin, J.A.: *Approaches to art therapy.* New York: Brunner/Mazel, 1987.

Sgroi, S.M.: *Handbook of clinical intervention in child sexual abuse.* Lexington, MA, Lexington Books, 1982.

Shapiro, J.: Moments with a multiple personality disorder patient. *Pratt Institute Creative Arts Therapy Review, 9:* 61-72, 1988.

Silvercloud, B.: Using art to express the unspeakable: A tool for intervenetion and therapy with the sexually-abused. *Art therapy: Still Growing.* Alexandria, VA, American Art Therapy Association, 86-90, 1983.

Simonds, S.L.: Sexual abuse and body image: Approaches and implications for treatment. *The Arts in Psychotherapy, 19*: 289-293, 1992.

Simonds, S.L.: *Bridging the silence: Nonverbal modalities in the treatment of adult survivors of childhood sexual abuse.* New York, W.W. Norton & Company, Inc., 1994.

Spring, D.: Symbolic language of sexually-abused, chemically dependent women. *American Journal of Art Therapy, 24*: 13-21, 1985.

Stember, C.J.: Change in maladaptive growth of abused girl through art therapy. *Art Psychotherapy, 5(2)*: 99-109, 1978.

Volgi-Phelps, V.: Letting the monsters out! *The Pointer, 29*: 35-40, 1985.

Yates, B.S., & Pawley, K.: Utilizing imagery and the unconscious to explore and resolve the trauma of sexual abuse. *Art Therapy, 7(1)*: 36-41, 1987.

Chapter 7

CASE EXAMPLE

The following represents an art therapy diagnostic assessment with a suspected sexual abuse survivor. Brian is an eight-year-old boy who was classified as emotionally disturbed. At a young age, he witnessed his father physically abuse his mother. Brian was also physically abused. In a session with his psychiatrist, Brian stated that "my daddy touches me." Although he verbally disclosed the sexual abuse to the psychiatrist, Brian has not discussed it since that time. He was admitted to day treatment due to emotional and behavioral difficulties at home and at school. Brian was referred to art therapy as means of dealing with his sexual abuse issues. It was also hoped that art therapy would aid in helping him express his feelings. Some of the graphic indicators mentioned earlier do appear in Brian's work, including, armless figures, defended figures, and images that had a sexual connotation (Johnston, 1979; Shengold, 1979; Johnson, 1987; Grubbs 1995).

The following represents the family genogram, Brian's time line, psychiatric summary, and psychological summary. The client's name and the names of the family members have been changed to maintain confidentiality. Brian's mother gave permission to print the artwork and diagnostic summary. Brian continued to participate in art therapy for several months after this evaluation. Some of his artwork from these sessions will be introduced.

IQ - 109

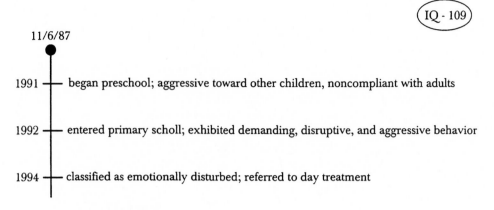

11/6/87

1991 —— began preschool; aggressive toward other children, noncompliant with adults

1992 —— entered primary scholl; exhibited demanding, disruptive, and aggressive behavior

1994 —— classified as emotionally disturbed; referred to day treatment

PSYCHIATRIC

I Attention Deficit Hyperactivity Disorder
Oppositional Defiant Disorder
Dysthymia
II Subtle learning disabilities
III Functional Enuresis (5-6 nights/week)

STRENGTHS
- intelligent
- strong reading abilities
- visual-perceptual skills

WEAKNESSES
- noncompliant/aggressive
- sexually acting out
- inattentive/poor focus

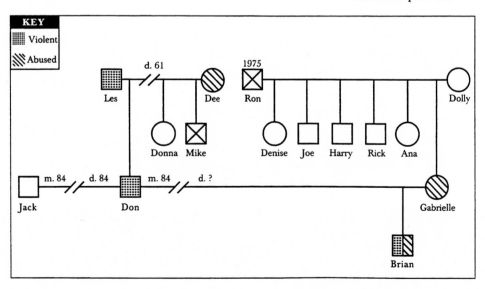

ART THERAPY DIAGNOSTIC ASSESSMENT

Name: Brian
DOB: 11/6/87
CA: 8 years; 2 months
Referral: referred by social worker because of sexual
                           abuse issues and aggression
Test Date: 2/13/95; 3/1/95; 3/6/95; 3/13/95; 3/27/95
Tests Administered: Kinetic House Tree Person Test (KHTP)
                           Kinetic Family Drawing (KFD)
                           Silver Drawing Test (STD)
                           Cognitive Art Therapy Assessment (CATA)
Administrant: Stephanie L. Brooke, MS, NCC Art Therapist

OBSERVATIONS, BEHAVIORAL IMPRESSIONS

Brian was an eight year old, white male referred to day treatment
because of aggressive and noncompliant behaviors in school and at
home. Currently, he lives with his mother. Sexual abuse allegations
have been made toward his father. Brian focused on violent themes
in his art work. During the session, he was very animated and verbal.
He enjoyed talking about his creations as he made them. When
the conversation approached sensitive areas, Brian became very
defended and closed. Overall, he worked well in paint and enjoyed
the process. On two occasions, he alluded to possible sexual abuse.

TEST RESULTS

Kinetic House-Tree-Person Test

   Brian began by drawing his house, possibly indicating a need
to survive, body needs or obsessions, or a need to have a home for
nurturing. He appeared to fall into Level One: Belonging to Life.
Brian was an approacher since his house resembled a prison

structure. This may represent a sanctuary, a place to keep one safe from people. The house was heavily shaded possibly suggesting anxiety. It had no doors or windows that may be indicating psychological inaccessibility. It was placed low on the page which may reveal feelings of insecurity, inadequacy, and possible defeatist attitudes.

Figure 7-1. House-Tree-Person Test

Next, Brian drew his person. The person's face was in profile possibly indicating paranoid tendencies. A large X was placed over the body of the person "born to be bad." This may suggest a need to control aggressive tendencies or may reveal an individual whom the drawer feels is ambivalent. The feet were diametrically opposed further suggesting opposing feelings. The right arm of the figure carried a sword whereas the left arm had been cut off above the elbow. Although a very defended figure, it suggested helplessness and possible concerns with bodily harm. The figure was armed and suspicious.

Last, Brian drew his tree. It was phallic shaped and heavily shaded, suggesting anxiety. It would be placed at Level 2: Belong to the body. He was an approacher since the tree was sexualized. Additionally, the tree was heavily defended containing weapons designed to kill President Clinton or anyone else who came close to the tree. The deep shading of the trunk may reveal pervasive anxieties.

Kinetic Family Drawing

Brian began the KFD by drawing the family pets, indicating some resistance to the task. The cat and the dog were fighting. Next, he drew himself on the far left side of the page, whereas his mother was drawn on the far right side of the page.

Figure 7-2. Kinetic Family Test

Additionally, several barriers existed between his mother and himself. This may indicate psychological distance. He drew a ball that he was going to catch but then erased it. He redrew the ball slightly behind his head saying that "it was out of my reach." This may reveal his method for dealing with competitive feelings. Both figures had claw-like hands, suggesting aggressiveness or possible defensiveness.

Silver Drawing Test

Predictive Drawing	11
Drawing from Observation	5
Drawing from Imagination	5

TOTAL SCORE: 21 out of a possible 45

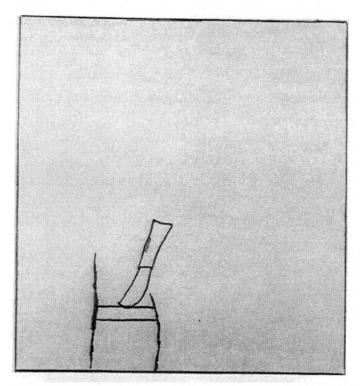

Figure 7-3. Silver Drawing Test - Drawing From Imagination

Brian's score of 21 placed him at the 33rd percentile for grade two with a T-score conversion of 45.53. He moved through the test quickly. His drawing of a knife cutting a bed recieved a score of one indicating negative themes.

Cognitive Art Therapy Assesment

Subtests	Scores
Clay Response	7-9 years; schematic stage Lowenfeld and Brittain
Drawing Response	7-9 years; schematic stage Lowenfeld and Brittain
Paint Response	7-9 years; schematic stage Lowenfeld and Brittain
Overall Response	**7-9 years; schematic stage** Lowenfeld and Brittain

Brian began working in clay. He squeezed the clay to create small differentiated shapes that he stuck together. He created a "powerful" figure that carried many weapons.

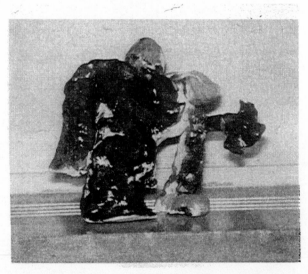

Figure 7-4. Cognitive Art Therapy Assesment - Clay Response

The pieces were not well joined. Brian did not incise features on to the clay. Essentially, he created the form and did not smooth out the clay afterwards. He seemed to enjoy the process. He started with the head, then created the body, legs, arms, and weapons. Again, he engaged in a violent theme: A person who destroys bad guys.

Figure 7-5. Cognitive Art Therapy Assesment - Clay Response

Later, he painted the face of the figure blue. After adding a touch of yellow paint to a shoulder, he painted the remainder of the figure black. The tip of the weapon was painted red. He was not invested in painting the figure and worked haphazardly to complete it. The figure was not completely covered with paint and the back of the figure had a watery colored appearance.

Next, Brian completed his pencil drawing. It contained five missiles with the word, Danger, written in each one. All of the missiles were directed at the moon to destroy it. A control box was placed between a few of the missiles. It had a detonator with the timer beginning at the point it was made. He used heavy pressure to create this drawing. Brian expressed that when the missals exploded, they caused one to bleed. When asked where one bled, he opened his legs and then moved his hand down to his calves. He seemed very defended at this point.

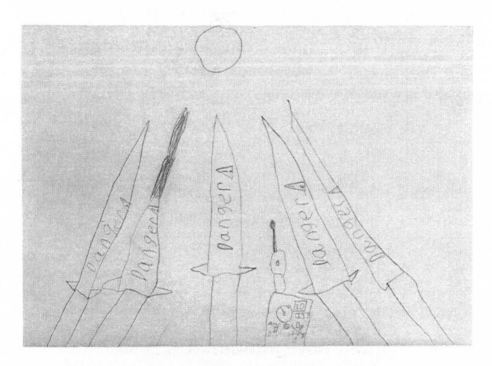

Figure 7-6. Cognitive Art Therapy Assesment - Pencil Response

Last, Brian completed a painting. This figure closely paralleled his clay piece. It was another defended figure that somewhat resembles a Power Ranger. He worked from the bottom of the page up, in a vertical manner. As his clay piece, this figure was lopsided suggesting instability. The legs appeared to be blocks that would make walking difficult. The figure had one long arm and another that had been cut off. The cut off arm was depicted in his KHTP. When he ran out of space at the top of the page, Brian added another page on top to finish the rest of the figure's helmet. He made the comment that the helmet came out of one's anus. The lower torso of the figure was painted red. The upper portion was mixed brown, yellow, and green. Brian used a mixture of horizontal and vertical brush strokes. He completed the picture quickly and armed the figure with a sword at its side.

Figure 7-7. Cognitive Art Therapy Assesment - Paint Response

RECOMMENDATIONS

Brian was very involved in the art process and expressed joy from exploring different art media. He showed a preference for black paint that may reveal depressive themes. Additionally, he displayed a marked vertical preference that may indicate assertiveness and possible hyperactivity. Overall, Brian worked in the schematic stage of development (7-9 years) according to Lowenfeld and Brittain (1987). This therapist highly recommends that Brian continue with individual art therapy. It is felt that the art materials and support of the therapist might provide an avenue for expressing his feelings. Painting may help him channel his aggressive energy. Also, art therapy may help him gain confidence in himself and improve his self-image. Stephanie L. Brooke, MS, NCC, Art Therapist

CONTINUED ART THERAPY

Several sexualized images appeared in Brian's work. The most provocative image was of a blue figure with a large penis pointed toward a person's derriere. I asked Brian to draw a picture of something that made him angry. When asked to describe his picture, Brian' replied, "It makes me angry when someone punches you in the butt."

Figure 7-8. Response to Angry Feelings

Brian perseverated on mazes. This may be an attempt to establish boundaries. Several phallic images emerged in his first maze. Additionally, Brian focused on toileting issues. The second maze is phallic shaped. Again, he appeared to be dealing with boundary issues, particularly in the number of pages he used. After connecting four pieces of paper, Brian stated that he would only add one more piece. This was a marked contrast to his earlier sessions when he went off the page or was unable to stop working.

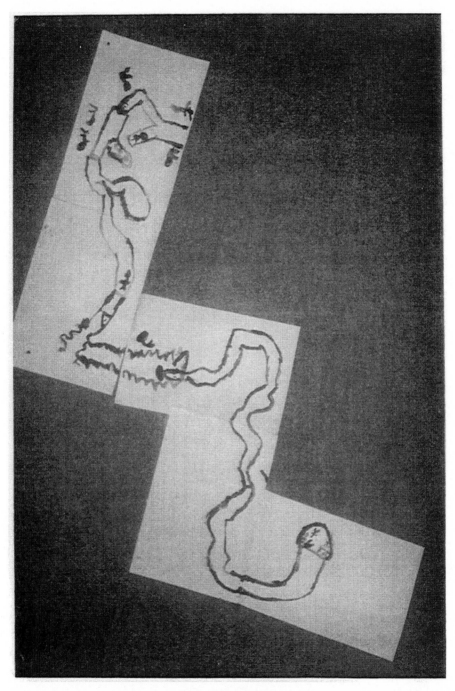

Figure 7-9. Maze 1

Figure 7-10. Maze 2

Violent themes were continually depicted in Brian's work. One image shows several bombs surrounding an individual. Often during his free time, Brian would draw violent pictures while in school. This posed a problem since some of his images were frightening the other children. As a result, Brian was given a notebook to draw his pictures

Figure 7-11. Bomb Drawing

on his own time. These pictures seem to be a way for Brian to deal with his strong, angry feelings.

Last, circles and wedges did appear in his work. According to Spring (1993), circles and wedges are common features in the work of sexual abuse survivors. In this particular drawing, Brian was drawing a tornado and stormy weather. This may relate to his feeling of being threatened or feeling unsafe.

Figure 7-12. Tornado Drawing

Although art therapy with Brian did not lead to a disclosure, it did help him come closer to sexual abuse issues without having to discuss them directly. Also, it provided Brian with a safe, acceptable outlet for expressing his feelings.

REFERENCES

Grubbs, G.A.: A comparative analysis of the sandplay process of sexually abused and nonclinical children. *The Arts in Psychotherapy, 22(5)*: 429-446, 1995.

Johnson, D.: The role of the creative arts therapies in the diagnosis and treatment of psychological trauma. *The Arts in Psychotherapy, 14*: 7-13, 1987.

Johnston, M.S.K.: The sexually mistreated child: Diagnostic evaluation. *Child Abuse & Neglect, 3:* 943-951, 1979.

Shengold, L.: Child abuse and deprivation: Soul murder. *Journal of the American Psychoanalytic Association, 27*: 533-559, 1979.

Spring, D.: *Shattered images: The phenomenological language of sexual trauma.* Chicago, IL, Magnolia Press, 1993.

Chapter 8

GROUP WORK
WITH SEXUAL ABUSE SURVIVORS

G roup therapy postulates that people learn and develop in the context of social interaction. Individuals may learn much about themselves by examining their rapport with others. For many mental health professionals, group work is the therapy of choice since many clients can be served simultaneously; therefore, it is more economical. Also, clients can develop their social skills. Generally, the rationale for the choice is that:

> the group often provides an awareness of the universality of one's experience, so that its members feel less negatively unique, less isolated, less alone. (Rubin, 1987, p. 305)

As a result, the group allows for immediate feedback and revelation of relationship patterns (Yalom, 1985). Additionally, some of the goals for group counseling are the development of trust in one's self and others, increasing self-confidence, and achieving self-knowledge. These goals appear to be particularly relevant when working with survivors of sexual abuse.

ART THERAPY GROUP THEORY

Rubin (1987) found that art mirrors and enhances the group process. "Promoting experiences of universality through the commonality that can be readily viewed in the content of the art productions, and the exploration of the here-and-now through art expression, make the marriage of group therapy and art therapy a dynamic union" (Rubin, 1987, p. 302). The use of art allows each member to participate in the group process.

Some therapists debate whether or not groups should be structured. Criticisms of structured groups largely focus on the use of themes (Waller, 1993). McNeilly (1983) contended that the use of themes uncovers powerful emotions too quickly; thereby, limiting the group process.

> What occurs in the majority of theme centered groups is a didactic process between separate members and the therapist... In this process, the therapist is seen as the provider or good mother who gives all the goodies. The therapist has here fallen into a dependency basic assumption from the start. He/she has agreed to feed the group and let it depend on him like a mother. (McNeilly, 1984, p. 7)

McNeilly argued that themes do emerge, over time, in nonstructured groups. Yalom (1985) supported McNeilly's (1984) statement that themes may be anti- therapeutic in that they may result in premature self-disclosure and may be too highly emotive for some group members.

On the other side of the debate is Liebmann (1986), who suggested the following rationale for structured groups (p. 11-12).

1. Many people have great difficulty in starting. A theme can give focus to begin somewhere.

2. Some initial themes can help groups understand what art therapy is all about. This is especially true if people in the group are not familiar with the approach, and see the art group in terms of former school art lessons or external aesthetic standards.

3. Some groups are very insecure and need structure if they are to operate at all.

4. There is often pressure of time. . . A group can get to the point more quickly if it focuses on a suitable theme.

5. Sharing a theme can help weld a group together.

6. Themes and exercises can be interpreted on many levels and used flexibly meet different needs. The group can be involved in the choice of theme if this is appropriate.

7. Certain themes can be useful in helping members of the group relate to each other.

8. Sometimes themes can help people get out of a "rut" by facilitating work and discussion which would otherwise not happen.

Generally, Liebman (1986) would begin group sessions by recapping the previous session, presenting an art activity, and concluding with a discussion of artwork . Although she was primarily responsible for choosing themes, groups that had been meeting for a longer period of time would take more responsibility in selecting a theme. Although providing structure may be helpful to some populations, sexual abuse survivors included, there are dangers in relying heavily on this approach to therapy:

> Art therapy isn't a piece of cake. An art therapist isn't there to provide projects. If she trusts the power of imagery and the healing forces within her client, she will allow her groups to flow naturally and organically. She will trust herself to be sensitive to their emergence so that she can foster their exploration and encourage the growth potential of the art therapy group and its individual members. (Wadeson, 1980, p. 158)

Wadeson (1980) discussed the advantages and disadvantages with structured and unstructured groups. Loosely-structured groups were not likely to foster cohesion yet can still be therapeutic for clients. Highly-structured groups offer more cohesion, trust, and discussion. The structural design of a group will depend on the population and group goals.

> A group can serve as an incubator for those who wish to molt the constraining shell of painful living patterns during the vulnerable process of developing new patterns. Since my belief is that much of life's problems stem from lack of acceptance of self, usually rooted in childhood family experience, my goal in the group is to foster an accepting, non-judgmental, caring milieu of the sort most people have never experienced. (Wadeson, 1980, p. 256).

In my experience leading sexual abuse survivors groups, providing structure initially helped to alleviate client concerns about the group process and creating art (Brooke, 1995a). I feel that structure is particularly helpful with survivors since they often deal with boundary issues. For many sexual abuse survivors, familial boundaries were unclear thereby causing confusion and doubt about their own perception of reality. By providing structure initially and setting clear boundaries, an environment conducive to trust, a key issue for sexual abuse survivors, can be maintained. Within the structured context, the group members have the freedom to choose media, themes, and activities. This freedom allows the members to feel a sense of empowerment thereby preventing dependence on the group leader(s)

Some therapists have found that art therapy is preferred to verbal approaches when working with sexual abuse survivors (Richards & Sealover, 1991; Waller, 1992). The main reason for this rationale is that sexual abuse survivors are lied to by their perpetrator. Words become misleading and mistrusted; therefore, verbal approaches to therapy may meet with more resistance (Waller, 1992). Through art, clients may disguise or symbolize their feelings and share as much or as little as they feel comfortable with at the time. Additionally, art therapy increases cohesion and self-esteem (Omizo & Omizo, 1989; Richards & Sealover, 1991; & Brooke, 1995a)

Given that many mental health professionals utilize group approaches , it seems feasible that combining the group approach with art therapy is an acceptable forum for treating sexual abuse survivors. Research reveals that group work is helpful in providing a sense of universality, nurturance, and trust (Hazzard, King, & Webb, 1986). Group work is effective for most sexual abuse survivors (Herman & Schatzow, 1984; Alexander et al., 1989; Friedrick, 1990; Wolf, 1993). Not only does group work improve peer relations, but it also addresses families' issues (Delvey, 1982; Alexander et al., 1989).

> The children expressed many times that the group was like a family and they acted out their family issues. Through the therapeutic process, they were able to change their ways of behavior and were able to adjust to the changes that were occurring in their own families as a result of therapy. (Wolf, 1993, p. 38)

Art therapy groups are a powerful mode of healing. The next section will focus on the use of art therapy groups with sexual abuse populations.

GROUP WORK WITH SEXUAL ABUSE SURVIVORS

I have conducted several art therapy groups for sexual abuse survivors. Initially, I conducted a pilot study to investigate the effectiveness of art therapy in raising levels of self-esteem (Brooke, 1995a). The study spanned eight weeks with the group members meeting for two hours per week. Eleven Caucasian, sexually abused women, ranging in age from 26 to 40 years, in Raleigh, North Carolina, participated in the study. Using a control-wait design, six women were assigned to the treatment group and five to the control group. The Culture-Free, Self-Esteem Inventory (SEI; Battle, 1981) was the standardized test administered in the pre and post sessions.

The group sessions were designed to enrich self-esteem. Participation was conditional in that the group member must currently have been in therapy. All work was placed on 8" by 11" white paper with a choice of the following media: crayons, water color, chalk, and pencil. Refer to Chapter 9 for examples of the member's artwork . The first 15 to 20 minutes was spent recapping the previous session. An hour was devoted to artwork, with the remainder of the session spent in discussion. Journal exercises accompanied the artwork.

By the time treatment was completed, the experimental group's self-esteem scores were significantly higher compared to their pretest scores. The study provided moderate evidence that art therapy, in a group format, improves some aspects of self-esteem, particularly with General and Social self-esteem scores.

It is possible that the lack of strong significant differences in SEI scores was due in part to the test instrument. The yes/no format is limited (Brooke, 1995b). Another instrument that utilizes a Likert scale may be more helpful in future investigations. The use of such a scale would give subjects more of a range when answering questions. Another factor that may contribute to the limited differences was the small sample size. The volunteer nature of the group limits also the generalizability of the findings.

In addition to the quantitative changes in self-esteem, qualitative changes did occur. Communications skills improved dramatically. Initially, many found it difficult, if not impossible, to discuss sexual abuse issues. Through art, group members found a way to communicate their feelings and later freely verbalized them. Trust also improved to the point that friendships continued after the conclusion of the group.

This study utilized a two-dimensional approach to art therapy. Three dimensional work, such as clay, is a particularly effective medium when working with sexual abuse survivors, since it lends itself to working through anger issues (Isaacs, 1983; Serrano, 1989; Powell & Faherty, 1990; Nez, 1991). Anderson (1995) conducted a group with incest survivors that exclusively worked with clay. In addition to empowering clients, Anderson (1995) felt that clay "would evoke emotional responses that would not be filtered through a client's intellectual (defensive) lenses. Thus, intellect and affect could be more easily integrated" (p. 415).

A group of female incest survivors participated in a nine-week program for clay work. The exact number of participants and demographic characteristics of the group were not discussed. Anderson (1995) combined clay work with journaling and discussion, as in the previous study. Family of origin issues, feelings about perpetrators, and representations of family of choice were just a few of the themes presented. The group concluded with an interesting exercise: Creating message tiles. These tiles were then assembled into one large piece.

A six-month, follow-up questionnaire revealed that the short-term art therapy clay group was an important event in the participants' lives. "They reported continuing positive progress and ongoing positive feelings about themselves as a result of participation in the art therapy group" (Anderson, 1995, p. 425). Anderson's work is a significant contribution to the field of art therapy because it utilizes a three-dimensional medium with this population. Clay is particularly powerful medium in dealing with anger issues: "Once some of the affect could be vented, clients could begin to move past the abuse experience(s) and toward an integration of affect and intellect and toward recovery" (Anderson, 1995, p. 415). As I have discovered, working through anger issues is the key to promoting self-esteem in sexual abuse survivors (Brooke, 1995a).

Corder (1990) and her colleagues conducted a pilot study using art therapy in conjunction with play therapy with a group of child survivors. Eight sexually-abused girls, ranging in age from 6 to 9, met for 20 group sessions that lasted five months. The focus was on cognitive relabeling of the experience and development of self-esteem. The group started with the sexual abuse coloring books that explored the fantasy and reality situations faced by sexually-abused children. For example, on the top, left-hand side of the page, the descriptor read, "Wouldn't it be nice if all touches were nice, right touches?" whereas the bottom half of the page read, "But the way it REALLY is..." (Corder et al., 1990, p. 245). The right-hand page focused on how children could change the situation. The Moving On and Getting Stronger Board Game allowed children to progress through a series of emotions as they healed and learned to protect themselves. For instance, children moved from Sad Valley to Mixed-Up

Mountain, to Learning Lake, to Positive Prairie, and finally to Safe Plain and Smart Mountain. Interviews with parents, teachers, and social workers were used to measure changes in the group. The researchers found that clients reported fewer sleep disturbances, demonstrated more compliant behavior, and became more verbally assertive. Although the study took some interesting and creative approaches to working with sexual abuse survivors, quantitative information was not presented on the changes made by the participants.

Powell and Faherty (1990) designed a 20-session, treatment plan for sexually-abused girls that combined group therapy and art therapy. The main goal of the plan was to strengthen the participants' ego. Self-portraits, puppet play, sex question bag, role play, and drawing perpetrators were just a few of the exercises listed by the authors. Although some artwork was presented, more time was spent on delineating the goals and plans for each session. Only qualitative outcomes were discussed. "The combination of the creative arts therapies and group process promotes positive, empowering, and dramatically corrective resolutions in the treatment of sexually-abused girls" (Powell and Faherty, 1990, p. 47).

Spring (1985) used drawings as a method for working with sexually-abused, chemically-dependent women. Fourteen women, ranging in age from 19 to 55 years, had admitted problems with alcohol and drugs. Spring (1985) found that the women would draw disembodied faces, bodies of water, and single red flowers. There was a consensus among the members that red flowers symbolized love and beauty; that people depicted the need for relationships and longing for family; and that water represented drinking alcohol, nurturing, peacefulness, and relaxation. No agreement was reached about the disembodied faces or lack of pupils. Spring (1985) asserted that she repeatedly saw two symbols in the artwork of sexual abuse survivors: eyes and wedges. The higher the level of posttraumatic stress, the greater the frequency of eyes and wedges (Spring, 1985). As Spring's work, a large body of the literature on sexual abuse examines common images in the work of survivors.

Waller (1992) utilized art therapy with a group of 15 adult female incest survivors ranging in age from 32 to 38 years. A control group, comprised of three women, participated in eight weekly individual therapy sessions. The remainder of the volunteers were broken down into two experimental groups that met for eight weeks for a duration of 90 minutes. One experimental group, consisting of seven members, utilized verbal techniques only, whereas the other experimental group, with five members, used art therapy techniques. Both treatment groups focused on social isolation, betrayal, trust issues, guilt, shame, anger, and confrontation of the perpetrator. The Curative Climate Instrument (Fuhrman, 1986) served as a pre and post test. This assessment measured a person's ratings of catharsis, cohesion, and insight (Waller, 1992).

Waller found that the art therapy group significantly increased in their value of insight as compared to the verbal and control groups. Although the verbal group increased their value of catharsis, the art therapy showed a significant increase in catharsis. The control group increased in their value of cohesion; yet, the art therapy group showed a significant increase in cohesion. On the other hand, the verbal group decreased in the level of cohesion. Although the sample sizes were limited, Waller (1992) found that art therapy was curative in that adult female incest survivors significantly increased their value of catharsis, cohesion, and insight. Since they were lied to as children, art may be a safer mode of self expression as compared to verbal approaches (Waller, 1992).

Some therapists used art therapy combined with other approaches in a group format. Hazzard and her colleagues (1986) worked with 11 sexually-abused adolescent girls, ranging in age from 11 to 16 years. All members were from lower income families, with 8 African-American females participating. The researchers found that art therapy was helpful in promoting emotional expression without intellectualization. The "draw a feeling exercise" seemed to be effective in ameliorating emotional constriction.

Levens (1994) used guided fantasy combined with art therapy when working with a group of sexually-abused adult females. All the participants were suffering from eating disorders. Levens (1994) presented the group with a fantasy and requested that they make an image in response to the fantasy. The exercise met with some resistance because a few members resented being told what to do. She found that several themes emerged from this process: rage towards the perpetrator, absent mother, feeling helpless, guilt, and blame.

Carozza and Hiersteiner (1982) identified five stages of growth when combining a group approach with art therapy: gathering, self-disclosure, regression, reconstruction, and ending. Using a 22-week treatment program, 6 to 10 sexually-abused victims, ranging in age from 9 to 17, participated in the study. The gathering stage was marked by assessments such as the Draw a Person and Kinetic Family Drawing. The self-disclosure stage began with a film that depicted the lives of three incest victims after which the members responded to the film in artwork. This stage was characterized by the increased cohesion and self-disclosure. During the regression stage, members worked in paint, which "can permit the externalization of intense inner conflict as well as permit a "free child" experience often denied victims because of adult responsibility inherent in the incest" (Carozza & Hiersteiner, 1982, p. 171). In the reconstruction stage, the members worked towards integration and resolution. Termination issues were dealt with in the last stage of therapy. Pre and post test results revealed a number of trends: increased figure size, illustrating the body, fewer erasures, decreased pencil pressure, improved quality of lines, less emphasis of clothing to hide the body, more central placement of figures on the page, and more realistic representation of self (Carozza & Hiersteiner, 1982).

Serrano (1989) utilized art therapy with six female incest survivors ranging in age from 19 to 36. During the initial sessions, members worked on safety, body, validation, and relationship issues. The middle stage focused on isolation and feelings of inadequacy. The termination stage dealt with body image, integration, and spontaneity. Serrano (1989) found that the members moved from feelings of being an isolated victim to an empowered survivor.

> Gradually, members became aware of their fractioned parts. They realized the absence of arms and legs represented the helplessness they felt. Awareness became the first step in recovery. (Serrano, 1989, p. 118)

Eye contact and body posture also improved as the group progressed. "At the end, although all members still had many issues of anger and sadness that came with the recognition of their losses, they had mastered their terror" (Serrano, 1989, p. 125). The art process allowed them to nurture themselves and one another.

McDonough and Love (1987) used a session of art therapy in the treatment of mothers and their sexually-abused children. In the beginning of the group, children drew their perpetrators and smeared their drawings with paint, paste, or markers. Some children drew their homes and put an X where the molestation took place.

Although mothers were initially uncomfortable with this process, they gradually came to understand their children, feel anger toward the abusers, and remember their own childhood abuse.

CONCLUSION

Studies which have examined the use of art therapy with sexual abuse survivors have been helpful in providing groundwork in the field; yet, there are limitations. For example, Yates et al. (1985) examined 15 dimensions of projective drawings with a group of sexual abuse survivors and a matched comparison group. The problem was that all of the children participating in this study were initially referred for psychiatric evaluation and treatment. All subjects were female. Although the authors stated that the comparison group consisted of disturbed girls who were not sexual abuse survivors, the representativeness of this group is questionable. Additionally, many survivors are unable to recall the abuse; therefore, it is possible that survivors were present in the comparison group. The range of age for both groups was extreme: Experimental (3.5 - 17 years) and Comparison (4 - 17 years). Some of the dimensions, "degree of immaturity," "control of impulses," "amount of confusion between love and anger," and "amount of confusion between sexual and aggressive impulses," may be inappropriate dimensions for the younger subjects. The developmental differences in the group may have affected the results.

One main weakness of all the studies mentioned in this chapter is that they focused only on females. In our society, there is less support for the male survivor due to the belief that males are "willing victims." Also, they are socialized to be responsible for initiating sexual behavior. Future research on art therapy groups with sexual abuse survivors should focus on male victims.

Another weakness inherent in most of the studies is the lack of information on quantitative changes in group members. The qualitative changes mentioned were helpful in providing insight into the group process and the benefits of art therapy. Focusing on quantitative changes, such as the Brooke (1995a) and Waller (1992) studies, will continue to provide validity evidence for the field of art therapy.

Although there is a debate whether or not to use structured groups, much of the literature indicates that therapists are providing structure when working with groups of sexual abuse survivors. This may be beneficial initially since survivors of sexual abuse traditionally have difficulty with boundary issues. Providing structure may promote trust and develop self-esteem.

From the research to date, art therapy with sexual abuse survivors appears to improve self-esteem, provide an outlet for threatening emotions, and foster problem solving skills. Since the abuse is difficult to talk about, art therapy offers a method for working through the issues related to the abusive situation in a safe, nonthreatening environment. Combining the group format with art provides members with a sense of universality with other sexual abuse survivors.

REFERENCES

Alexander, P.C., Neimeyer, R.A., Follette, V.M., Moore, M.K., & Harter, S.: A comparison of group treatments of women sexually-abused as children. *Journal of Consulting and Clinical Psychology, 57(4)*: 479-483, 1989.

Anderson, F.E.: Catharsis and empowerment through group claywork with incest survivors. *The Arts in Psychotherapy, 22(5)*: 413-427, 1995.

Battle, J.: *Culture-Free SEI self-esteem inventories for children and adults.* Seattle, WA, Special Child Publications, 1981.

Brooke, S.L.: Art therapy: An approach to working with sexual abuse survivors. *The Arts in Psychotherapy, 22(5)*: 447-466, 1995a.

Brooke, S.L.: A critical review of Battle's Culture-Free Self-Esteem Inventory, *Measurement and Evaluation in Counseling and Development, 27 (4)*: 248-252, 1995b.

Carozza, P.M., & Hiersteiner, C.L.: Young female incest victims in treatment: Stages of growth seen with a group art therapy model. *Clinical Social Work Journal, 10(3)*: 165-175, 1982.

Corder, B.F., Haizlip, T., and DeBoer, P.: A pilot study for a structured, time-limited therapy group for sexually-abused pre-adolescent children. *Child Abuse & Neglect, 14*: 243-251, 1990.

Delvey, J.: Parenting errors and their correction in group psychotherapy. *American Journal of Psychotherapy, 36*: 523-535, 1982.

Friedrick, W.N.: *Psychotherapy of sexually-abused children and their families.* New York, W.W. Norton, 1990.

Fuhrman, A.: *The Curative Climate Instrument.* Salt Lake City, UT, Author, 1986.

Hazzard, A., King, H.E., & Webb, C.: Group therapy with sexually-abused adolescent girls. *American Journal of Psychotherapy, XL(2)*: 213-223, 1986.

Herman, J., & Schatzow, E.: Time-limited group therapy for women with a history of incest. *International Journal of Group Psychotherapy, 34*: 605-616, 1984.

Isaacs, M.: Beyond throwing clay: An art therapist's model for anger expression and treatment. *Art therapy: Still growing.* Alexandria, VA, American Art Therapy Association, 39-41, 1983.

Levens, M.: The use of guided fantasy in art therapy with survivors of sexual abuse. *The Arts in Psychotherapy, 21(2)*: 127-133, 1994.

Liebmann, M.: *Art therapy for groups: A handbook of themes, games, and exercises.* Cambridge, MA, Brookline Books, 1986.

McDonough, H., & Love, A.J.: The challenge of sexual abuse: Protection and therapy in a child welfare setting. *Child Welfare, LXVI(3)*: 225-235.

McNeilly, G.: Directive and non-directive approaches in art therapy. *The Arts in Psychotherapy, 10(4)*: 211-219, 1983. (Reprinted in Incscape, December, 1984).

Nez, D.: Persephone's return: Archetypal art therapy and the treatment of a survivor of abuse. *The Arts in Psychotherapy, 18(2)*: 123-130, 1991.

Omizo, M.M., & Omizo, S.A.: Art activities to improve self-esteem among native Hawaiian children. *Journal of Humanistic Education & Development, 27*: 167-176, 1989.

Powell, L. & Faherty, S.L.: Treating sexually-abused latency age girls. *The Arts in Psychotherapy, 17*: 35-47, 1990.

Richards, J.B., & Sealover, I.E.: Counseling techniques for sexually-abused children. *TACD Journal, Spring*: 47-51, 1991.

Rubin, J.A.: *Approaches to art therapy.* New York, Brunner/Mazel, 1987. Serrano, J.S.: The arts in therapy with survivors of incest. In H. Wadeson (Ed), *Advances in art therapy.* New York, Harper & Row, 1989.

Spring, D.: Symbolic language of sexually-abused, chemically dependent women. *American Journal of Art Therapy, 24*: 13-21, 1985.

Wadeson, H.: *Art Psychotherapy.* New York, John Wiley & Sons, 1980.

Waller, C.S.: Art therapy with adult female incest survivors. *Art Therapy: Journal of the American Art Therapy Association, 9(3)*: 135-138, 1992.

Waller, D.: *Group interactive art therapy: Its use in training and treatment.* New York, Routledge, 1993.

Wolf, V.B.: Group therapy of young latency age sexually-abused girls. *Journal of Child and Adolescent Group Therapy, 3(1)*: 25-39, 1993.

Yalom, I.: *The Theory and Practice of Group Psychotherapy.* New York, Basic Books, 1985.

Yates, A., Beutler, L.E., & Grago, M.: Drawings by child victims of incest. *Child Abuse and Neglect, 9(2)*: 183-189, 1985.

Chapter 9

ART THERAPY WITH A GROUP OF
SEXUAL ABUSE SURVIVORS

GROUP DESIGN:

The following intervention was developed to promote psychological growth and healing. Specifically, the group members
were given the opportunity to express feelings through art and
writing. Participation was conditional in that the group member
must have been currently in therapy. Freedom of expression was
encouraged. All work was placed on 8" by 11" white paper with
a choice of the following media: crayons, water colors, chalk, and
pencil. Participants signed release forms stating that I could publish
their artwork as long as they remained anonymous.

I provided positive feedback on artwork and facilitated the
discussion. Each session was two hours long and spanned
eight weeks. The first hour was spent on the art activity, while the
remaining hour focused on discussion. The women volunteered
to share their art experiences during this time. Journal entries were
discussed on a volitional basis.

SAMPLE:

The treatment sample consisted of 6 women from Raleigh, North
Carolina. All subjects were white, middle-class females. The average
age was 30, with a range from 26 to 40 years. All subjects
volunteered to participate in the group.

SESSION 1:

The first session opened up with an icebreaker: Each person

interviewed a partner and then presented the person to the group. Specifically, they were to find out what the person's hopes and fears were for the group. Continued healing, dealing with feelings, and bonding with others were among the hopes of the group. The group's fears centered on creating art, feeling alone, trusting new people, and safety. The issue of confidentiality was stressed as part of the facilitator's and members' responsibilities. Next, the group goals and membership responsibilities were written on a flip chart and discussed.

The opening art exercise was "If you were a color, what color would you be?" Purple, green, black, and rainbow colors characterized group drawings. Using water color, crayon, and pencil, a variety of images were created. Vases, amorphous images, hearts, and triangles were the shapes drawn.

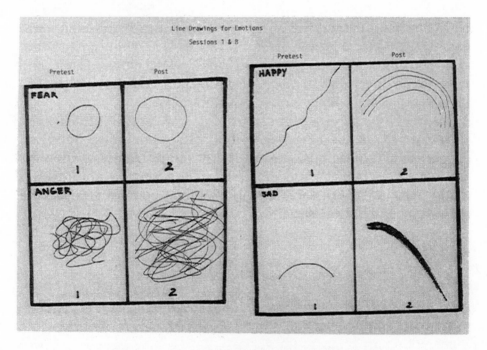

Figure 9-1. Line drawing for emotions (sessions 1&8)

Triangle and heart images have been associated with the drawings of sexually abused adolescents (Sidun & Rosenthal, 1987; Cohen & Phelps, 1985; Spring, 1993). Their journal exercise asked "What was it like to represent yourself as a shape and color?"

It wasn't like too much of anything. It actually seemed unrelated to me, external, as though I really could have made any selection, put down any color or shape, just to have an answer. But once I settled on purple, it seemed to fit. Triangle won by default, a pennant shaped triangle with a right angle. Pure, and flat on the bottom, yeah.

It felt good to draw a multisided shape with many shapes and colors inside because that's who I am. Each part of me has her own color and shape.

My color is purple and green swirling out into haze with black at the center. My feelings: I can't really say-it's just me-black center with many layers of calm (purple) growth (green) surrounding it... My shape is a black spatter. My feelings-some places I overextend, some I don't extend enough and most of the time I'm just all over the place.

Shape I'd like to be; crystal vase-smooth curves-no rough edges beautiful, graceful, poised. Felt a bit uncomfortable when we started the art, but got into it more as we went on. *Color I'd like to be*: Rainbow: pink-love-blue-spirituality, green-healing, yellow & red-strength, happiness. I also envision these colors in a string, braid-interwoven-strength.

According to Klepsch and Logie (1982), the colors depicted in these drawings may represent controlled reactions and self-restraint. Obviously, from the last quotation, people use different colors to represent different emotions. In subsequent survivor groups, I developed a rainbow chart which serves as a more accurate index of the artist's affective associations with color. The chart contains several colors to which the client is asked to write how each particular color makes them feel.

The next exercise focused on drawing lines for happiness, sadness, anger, and fear. Happiness lines resembled sine waves. Tear drops or upside-down U's were drawn for sadness while rash and random lines indicated anger. Circles or V's were used to depict fear. When asked how they related to the lines, group members wrote:

Happiness is gentle, easy going, sort of soft. Sadness is a steady decline, bumpy along the way, lasts longer than happiness. Anger is jagged, pointed, up and down, in and out, hard to hold. Fear is penetrating, sharp, with plenty of room for entry at the top, but no exit.

Fear is being closed in, lack of freedom to be who I truly am-I feel trapped. Sadness-it is always a tear for me-never without a tear. Happiness is a circle, its being whole and well rounded-maybe one day. Anger is always sharp, it can and does destroy-never to be released without watching myself.

Anger-a mass of confusion because everyone wants to handle the anger differently and we become overwhelmed. Fear-a circle represents fear because it never ends. Circles also represent secrecy.

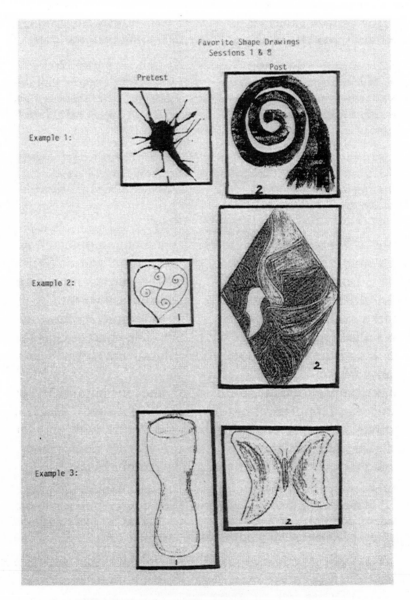

Figure 9-2. Favorite shape drawings (sessions 1&8)

The shapes and line drawings for this session served as a baseline. They will be compared to similar drawings in Session 8 (Baseline (pretest) drawings are labeled "1" and Session 8 (post) drawings are labeled "2").

SESSION 2:

The art activity for this session focused on the creation of a self-portrait; an indication of the woman's present emotional state. The group pasted a mirror on the center of the page. They were instructed to look in the mirror and draw or paste magazine images around the mirror that represented self. Then they were to write something on the page using their nondominant hand.

More than the other exercises, the self-portraits utilized magazine images. There were a variety of images: Eyes, masks, children, and families. Figure 9-3 was the only one that did not use magazine images. The theme of lost innocence was present in most drawings. The masks, for the group, represented the dark side, untrustworthiness, or denial. One member wrote:

> To most of those who know me, I am a very happy, together person. And I don't really think they are totally wrong. There is a lot of me that enjoys my life. But there is also this little girl who thinks that no one likes her and is very ashamed and sad. Oh... but I do cover up well. But not well enough. Big XXX also knows that she is not well liked. It's hard to hide from yourself.

Eyes stood for knowing, seeing more than most children, and pain. One person's self-portrait focused only on her eyes. Disembodied eyes are a common feature in the work of survivors (Spring, 1993). Another woman drew an abstract drawing (a swirl of lines attached to the upper portion of the mirror) and wrote with her nondominant hand, "HELP ME HATE." The topic of anger, let alone its expression, is very difficult for most survivors. Although they have much to be angry about, most in the group did not feel comfortable expressing anger. Others had pushed it so far out of consciousness that they were having difficulty getting in touch with angry feelings or denied having them. One of the group members commented on this in her journal:

> I guess from each person I found something to relate to. It was good to hear denial discussed, and by someone who seems to have a lot of

memories. It's so hard to tell what's real, what to trust, and to shut out your mind when it's telling you over and over again you are nuts, while every cell in your body seems to be screaming out at you it happened, it happened, it happened.

Figure 9-3. Self-portrait (session 2)

Body image was an important issue for most group members. The self-portrait activity touches on this. Perhaps a future group can incorporate an art activity that addresses this concern more fully. For the survivor of sexual abuse, poor body image is representative of underlying emotional problems and is potentially destructive. Some of the women in the group were concerned about their weight. One person wrote:

> The pig and the marshmallow represent the fat me. I hate my weight problem. I know that people think of heavy people differently. They are valued less. When I can't control what goes into my mouth, I feel that I can't control any other facet of my life. I'm feeling totally out of control and an out of control person is a sad person.

Blume (1990) reported that survivors will manipulate their body size to protect themselves from sexually-oriented responses: "A survivor might choose to be large and unapproachably powerful, or invisible and childlike in her thinness, or perfect through bulimia" (p. 196-197). When power is taken in the form of a sexually abusive relationship, many women will attempt to gain power by manipulating their body size. The tie between sexual abuse and subsequent eating disorders is strong:

> Women suffering from eating disorders are telling us, in the only way they know how, that something is going seriously wrong with their lives as they take on the rights and perogatives of male society. (Chernin, 1985, p. 19)

The common emotional theme was that of sadness. The feelings of lost innocence or lost love were common. One after-effect of abuse is depression, which many of the group members were struggling to overcome. Guilt, shame, self-blame, and low self-esteem contribute to depression. The loss of control and power also are factors. As Freire (1981) found in the drawings of dispossessed workers, oppressive themes in their artwork indicated barriers to empowerment.

SESSION 3:

The family drawing was the most difficult activity for the group to complete. Most people used pencil for this activity which is characteristic of controlled reactions (Robbins, 1987). Isolation was a common theme in most drawings. Also, the mother was shown doing housework while the father was displayed relaxing, drinking, or watching television. Some of the survivors in the group were also children of

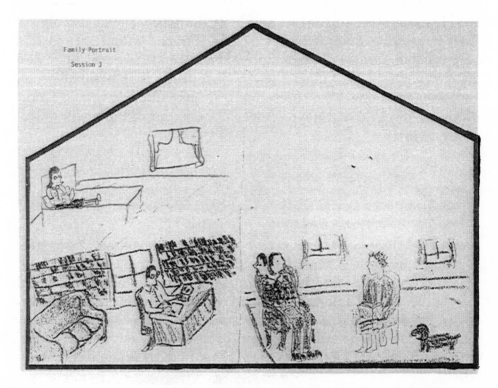

Figure 9-4. Family portrait (session 3)

alcoholic parents, which was depicted in the drawings. Often, the group drew themselves in their bedrooms, where they seemed to spend most of their time. One individual did not draw herself at all. Omissions like this are indicative of low self-esteem and are a feature associated with abused children (Schorstein & Derr, 1978; Cohen & Phelps, 1985). Discussion of the activity led to the topic of role reversal: Many members of the group had to function in the role of parent and caretaker for their siblings and their parents. For some, the role was of psuedo-wife:

> Mistress and secret lover to my father. I earned my keep by being sold to his friends and posing for movies and pictures.

> I remember my childhood as a happy time. I don't know if that's the way it was or the way I choose to remember it.

> I felt fear, anger, grief-Fear of the reaction, anger at being afraid and angry at how Dad had affected my life and my feelings about myself-Grief at losing the picture I had of my family.

Many described their family as outwardly perfect, yet they carried the burden of the truth. Drinking problems, marital conflicts, and the sexual abuse were the house secrets. The roles of "little mother" and "father's confidant" made them feel responsible for keeping the family together. Generally, the fathers were described as engendering feelings of disgust, hatred, and rage. The mothers were represented as hardworking and unaware of the abuse.

SESSION 4:

This session opened up with the homework exercise: Draw a tree. Some theorists feel that the tree is characteristic of the individual (Burns & Kaufman, 1970, 1972; DiLeo, 1970, 1973). Two people drew slanted trees which may indicate instability. It should be mentioned that these two individuals were struggling with vague memories. When asked what they were thinking about when drawing the tree, they mentioned that they were trying to regain the memories of sexual abuse. One drawing focused only on the tree trunk, with a knothole, and large roots. For her, the roots represented strength and the knothole a safe place. Long roots were shown in another drawing of a fruit tree. For this person, the fruit represents giving back to life and the long roots stability and strength. Fruit trees appear to be common with this population and may reveal a need for nurturance.

Many group members still suffer from nightmares. The art activity for this session focused on dreams and personal interpretation. Nightmares often spark the first memories of the abuse (Davis, 1990). For most of the group, memories were still sparse. Dream work may be one method for uncovering memories about the abuse. "Horror-filled, terrifying, full of images of entrapment and violence-they [nightmares] represent the themes of incest" (Blume, 1990, p. 98). In addition, Blume (1990) noted that dreams of being chased, threatened, or trapped were typical for survivors.

Pencil and crayon were the common media used. Again, this suggests more controlled reactions (Klepsch & Logie, 1982). Images of violence, confusion, and Satanism were represented in the dreams for this group. One person came from a family that practiced Satanism and her abuse was ritualistic. Another person wrote:

> I dreamed that my ex-husband was trying to kill me. I know he would actually never try to kill me, but there is a big part of me that is very afraid

of his power as a manipulator. I think that is the symbolism. It is that being married to him was destroying me little by little-murder of the soul instead of the body. I didn't trust my own feelings. Until I got out of the marriage, I didn't know that I was such a victim of his manipulation.

Figure 9-5. Dream drawing (session 4)

Another member drew her perpetrator and her uncle with a mass of a lines at the top (Brooke, 1995). In addition, the shading at the top

Figure 9-6. Tree drawing (session 4)

may indicate insecurity with the environment or anxiety (Burns & Kaufman, 1970, 1972; DiLeo, 1970, 1973). Another person drew a shadowy figure standing in the doorway of her bedroom. She is not sure if this is a dream or a memory. Blume (1990) stated that some survivors will dream about the abuse, but it may be slightly distorted.

> A faceless young man, matching the memories I've been able to grasp of my father. Blank, like my mind when I think of him... What did the cane signify? Was it his helplessness or mine? Maybe it was both. He became ugly with the cane, old and ugly. I don't know maybe the cane represents some sort of power. It was the old man who had sex with me, he was the one...

Many members of the group continued to record and interpret their dreams. I suggested some strategies to help them: Telling yourself that you will remember the dream, repeatedly, before you go to sleep, using a tape recorder in the morning, or repeating the sequences of the dream. Dreams represent unconscious elements in some theoretical perspectives. If the elements are too dangerous in their original form, they are symbolized. The group was encouraged to focus on the symbols of the dream and the predominant feeling associated with it. Additionally, it was suggested that if they were stuck on a symbol, to personify it as a method of interpretation.

SESSION 5:

Due to our socialization process, many women have difficulty expressing feelings of anger. Sexual abuse survivors are no exception. Part of a woman's responsibility, in our culture, is to be good by staying in control (Bepko & Krestan, 1990). Often there is a high price for maintaining control. The silence that surrounds sexual abuse has dire consequences for survivors. It is not surprising that survivors suffer from a variety of somatic complaints. Migraine headaches have often been associated with suppressed anger (Blume, 1990). Although survivors have much to be angry about, they have been robbed of this emotion by social injunctions or by the power of the perpetrator. "Drawing your Monster" was a method to help them release feelings of anger, guilt, and fear through art.

One individual drew a series of pornographic images with squares and triangles covering the genitals. Her father often left pornographic magazines and videos around the house. Another person drew an abusive incident: Her coach would take her in the alley and abuse her. She depicted herself in this drawing as killing her monster, demonstrating her angry feelings (Brooke, 1995). One woman did a collage of male body parts in the framework of a penis. All the eyes in this work were blocked out: She felt that this represented her fear of men. Another person drew her perpetrator as two-headed: one head smiling that was presented to the world and the other having features of a devil.

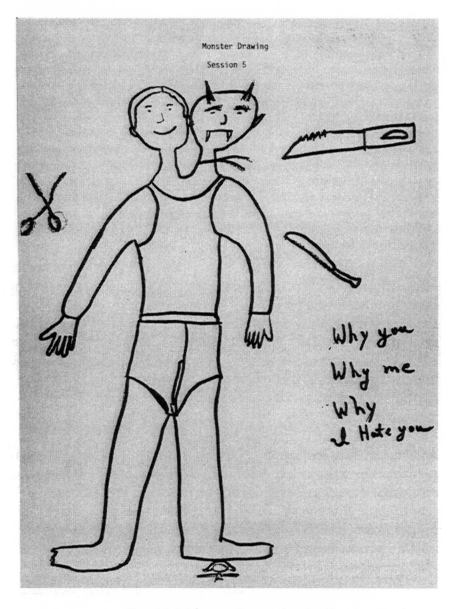

Figure 9-7. Monster drawing (session 5)

She shows this figure stepping on her. Her small size in comparison to the "monster" may indicate low self-esteem (Burns & Kaufman, 1970, 1972; DiLeo, 1970, 1973). She expressed her anger by drawing a variety of cutting instruments surrounding this figure and writing "I hate you."

> I have too many monsters to contemplate. Most of the time they don't bother me. But sometimes that depression monster takes the first bite and it's painfully easy for the others to do what harm they can. I can feel moment by moment the sinking feeling as they pull me down into darkness and many times it seems the only way out is to RAGE. Unfortunately, now the person who suffers in silence has a new monster: Misdirected anger and rage. To me this picture represents all the long-burried anger, it represents confusion. I went back to the first assignment, drawing emotions in lines, and then I looked at this monster picture. The most prevalent lines are those of fear and anger. The sky is drawn in lines of sadness. I don't see any lines of happiness. I guess that's because there is no happiness in this monster, only anger and fear, the magnitude of which frightens me, but also brings a sense of relief. I have no idea what to do with all this anger, but there is somehow a sense of comfort in learning I am capable of feeling beyond regret and depression.

This activity only revealed the tip of the iceberg with respect to the issue of anger. Franklin (1992) stressed that anger is a strongly avoided emotion; yet, the key to developing positive self-esteem is dependent upon acknowledgment and expression of this emotion. Clay is another medium that will allow the client to work through feelings of anger. Subsequent groups included a second session devoted to anger issues using clay as a medium.

SESSION 6:

Drawing wishes can provide the opportunity not only to express fantasy, but to express fears. Malchiodi (1990) asserted that what a person wishes for represented what she has lost or fears losing. The images in these drawings centered on the wish for an improved body image, intimate relationships, a happy childhood, power, and freedom. The group members utilized a variety of media: Magazine images, pencil, and crayon.

> My wish is all about me. It is the very essence of me-the little girl who doesn't love herself and thinks no one else will either. Because I was taught that I had to do something for someone to love me, I like myself for all that I do but not for who I am. I'm a nice person, but I can't love myself just for

being me. That's weird, but the sum is less than the parts. I'm honest, open, caring, a good mom, a great employee, and nice to people, but I feel I'm unlikable, unlovable. I wish more than anything that I could change that. I really just wish I could say and mean, "I love myself."

Figure9-8. Wish drawing (session 6)

The wish is me-parts of a face-one eye, a lip-reflections of the partial regaining of self and emotion. My birds are in the picture. That's the real wish, to be free and easy as birds gliding in front of the warm sun on an autumn afternoon; going where instinct takes them, their cries lifted far and unencumbered through the air; weightless.

Using the same principles as dream interpretation, wish drawings can be decoded to uncover the meaning associated with the images. It is stressed that the interpretation is solely in the hands of the artist. The role of the counselor or facilitator is to provide techniques for decoding the symbols. For instance, have the person become the image in the drawing: If you are the bird in this drawing, what are you experiencing, feeling, or thinking about.

SESSION 7:

This session opened up with the favorite animal drawing. The intention of this exercise was to see how the favored characteristics of the animal related to the self. One person drew birds as representative of the freedom that she craves. The birds are high above the mass of confusion; similar to the feelings of disassociation she experiences when her life becomes complicated. Another individual pasted a series of animals on her picture: Minnie Mouse, eagle, monkey, cougar, raccoon, deer, and owl. Above the raccoon she wrote "Twilight mischief." She felt that the image of the deer and its reflection in the water clearly related to her feelings. She wrote, "We are not who we are but how we're seen." She stressed that how she feels about herself is dependent upon how others view her. This drawing was multifaceted; it represented different characteristics of herself. One woman drew a cat, her favorite animal. She likes the independent nature of the cat as well as its capacity to be friendly and seek attention. These are goals she strives for in her life.

The activity for this session focused on a free drawing. The goal was to free up imagery and increase self-esteem by creating a unique product. One woman focused on pornographic images, the circles and squares were the first ideas that came to mind. Another woman drew a series of small circles which resembled the Yin/Yang symbol. Some circles are more complete than others and one is shaded out. For her, it represented the struggle between happiness and depression. Another drawing focused on a woman crying, teardrops, and a shattered heart (Brooke, 1995). A jumble of words appeared on one

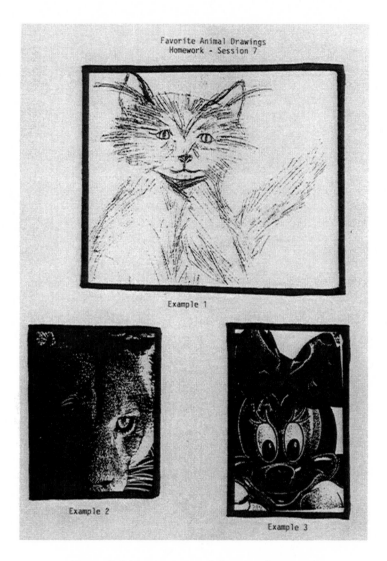

Figure 9-9. Favorite animal drawing (session 7)

corner of the picture that represented her confused thoughts about the abuse. Another woman drew herself inside the womb. For her it was a safe, happy place. Images of a happy, peaceful childhood predominated another free drawing.

Figure 9-10. Free drawing (session 7)

SESSION 8:

The art activity focused on redoing the baseline exercise. It was interesting for the group to compare their drawings to the first exercise. Most changes occurred in the happiness quadrant. The sine waves were replaced by rainbows or "curly q's." The other quadrants remained similar to the original drawings. Shapes did change: Heart to stained-glass diamond; black splatter to a spiral; and a vase to a butterfly to name a few (see Figures 9-1 & 9-2). Generally, the group felt more positive about the new shapes that they created.

For the remainder of the session, the group decided what they wanted to do. Most people wanted to spend their time in discussion. They talked about what group they thought about joining next, how they would stay in touch, and what they felt was valuable from this group. Most people found it beneficial to express their feelings through drawing.

I found that art therapy in a group setting can be worthwhile for promoting self-awareness and improved sense of self. Combining Psychoanalytic, Cognitive, and Group approaches to art therapy seemed beneficial for growth and healing. The art activities allowed for the expression of a variety of emotions in a safe environment. Also, it provided an opportunity for empowerment and developing trust in others. For other populations that share similar feelings of low self-esteem (eating disorders), this intervention may be beneficial for them.

REFERENCES

Bepko, C., & Krestan, J.: *Too good for her own good: Breaking free from the burden of female responsibility.* New York, Harper & Row, 1990.

Blume, E.S.: *Secret survivors: Uncovering incest and its after effects in women.* New York, John Wiley & Sons, 1990.

Brooke, S.L.: Art therapy: An approach to working with sexual abuse survivors. *The Arts in Psychotherapy, 22(5)*: 447-466.

Burns, R.C., & Kaufman, S.H.:. *Kinetic family drawings (K-F-D).* New York, Brunner/Mazel, 1970.

Burns, R.C., & Kaufman, S.H.: *Actions, styles, and symbols in kinetic family drawings (K-F-D).* New York, Brunner/Mazel, 1972.

Chernin, K.: *The hungry self: Women, eating, and identity.* New York, Time Books, 1985.

Cohen, F.W., & Phelps, R.E. Incest markers in children's artwork. *Arts in Psychotherapy, 12*: 265-284, 1985.

Davis, L.: *The courage to heal workbook: For women and men survivors of child sexual abuse.* New York, Harper & Row, 1990.

DiLeo, J.H.: *Young children and their drawings.* New York, Brunner/Mazel, 1970.

DiLeo, J.H.: *Children's drawings as diagnostic aids.* New York, Brunner/ Mazel, 1973

Franklin, M.:. Art therapy and self-esteem. *Art Therapy, 9 (2)*: 78-84, 1992.

Freire, P.: *Pedagogy of the oppressed.* New York, Herder and Herder, 1971.

Klepsch, M., & Logie, L.: *Children draw and tell: An introduction to the projective uses of children's human figure drawings.* New York, Brunner/Mazel, 1982.

Malchiodi, C.A.: *Breaking the silence: Art therapy with children from violent homes.* New York, Brunner/Mazel, 1990.

Robbins, A.: *The artist as therapist.* New York, Human Sciences Press, 1987.

Schorstein, H.M., & Derr, J.: The many applications of kinetic family drawings in child abuse. *British Journal of Projective Psychology and Personality Study, 23*: 33-35, 1978.

Sidun, N.M., & Rosenthal, R.H.: Graphic indicators of sexual abuse in draw-a-person tests of psychiatrically hospitalized adolescents. *The Arts in Psychotherapy, 14*: 25-33, 1987.

Spring, D.: *Shattered Images: The phenomenological language of sexual trauma.* Chicago, Magnolia Press, 1993.

Chapter 10

ART THERAPY
WITH SEXUALLY-ABUSIVE FAMILIES

CHARACTERISTICS OF SEXUALLY ABUSIVE FAMILIES

Sexual abuse crosses gender, cultural, and socioeconomic barriers which indicates that the causes of sexual abuse are dynamic and complex. Power processes within the family contribute to the occurrence of sexual abuse. According to Forward and Buck (1989), sexual abuse originates in families where there is isolation, secrecy, and lack of respect for women. These factors serve to maintain power of the perpetrator and precipitate the occurrence of sexual abuse.

It is the result of the misuse of familial bases of power, that the processes within the family lead to an abuse of power. A perpetrator is able to abuse legitimate bases of power in order to engage the child in a sexual relationship. For instance, the reward power is abused when the perpetrator withholds love and attention from a child not willing to engage in a sexual relationship. Herman (1981) noted that this is characteristic of abusive fathers who will only provide love and attention within the context of a sexually-abusive relationship.

The family is the primary socializing agent for a child. Parents are viewed as omnipotent because they are believed to be experts, role models, and have the power reward or punish the child's behaviors. Parental power is the decisive agent in a child's life; therefore, "the child learns that power and authority dominate human relationships-not trust and tolerance" (Allport, 1979 p. 299). This has a significant impact on survivors. Both male and female survivors learn to distrust their view of reality.

Other familial processes are linked to sexual abuse. The social-psychological model holds that "frustration and stress are important variables associated with child abuse" and that this stress comes from several sources: marital disputes, too many children, unemployment, social isolation, unwanted children, and a "problem child" (Justice & Justice, 1976, p. 46). Rapid life change is a precipitating factor in abuse. Along the same lines, the environmental stress model attributes abuse to factors such as poverty, poor education, and occupational stress. Individuals who support this theory assert that abuse is associated with the lower class, but it is known that abuse occurs in all economic classes (Justice & Justice, 1976).

> Perhaps because incest is so deeply enmeshed in culture, psychology, and sexuality, an analysis of environmental factors alone cannot tell us as much as we need to know. (Breines & Gordon, 1983, p. 528)

Essentially, stress caused by poverty, unemployment, alienation, alcohol and drug abuse, and a breakdown in the family structure distinguish sexually abusive families (Justice & Justice, 1976). Although these models view abuse as resulting from factors of frustration, it is my view that abuse results from an effort to gain power. From the perspective of the perpetrator, these factors which cause stress may lead to feelings of powerlessness. Men who are powerless in the workplace "often have a greater need to think of women as inferior; almost everybody needs to feel superior to somebody as part of his or her definition of self, and we [men] spend a lot of aggressive energy treating women consciously or unconsciously, as an underclass" (Astrachan, 1986, p. 18). For this reason, the perpetrator compensates for feelings of powerlessness by maintaining absolute power over his/her family and abuses the bases of power granted by the dominant culture in order to satisfy his/her needs.

Gomez-Schwartz and colleagues (1990) believe that sexual abuse often ensued from disruptions in the family, unclear boundaries, and isolation. The family structure model focused on alliances, coalitions, enmeshments, and disengagements among family members (Justice & Justice, 1976). The concept of coalitions related to the finding that illegitimate and unwanted children are at high risk for abuse (Gomez-Schwartz et al., 1990). According to Hansen and colleagues (1983), sexually abusive families fall within either the enmeshed or disengaged-chaotic categories. In the enmeshed families, perpetrators turn to children when the marriage begins to fail as opposed to seeking sexual satisfaction outside the family. Perpetrators will verbalize love and caring feelings toward the victim. Children are not a threat to the perpetrator and they place him/her in a powerful position, one which may not be attainable if sexual relationships are sought outside the home. On the other hand, Hansen (1983) described the disengaged-chaotic family as having indiscriminate sexual relationships with family and nonfamily members. There is more potential for violence in this family. In both cases, sexual abuse was the result of an abuse of power since parents are in a position of power and the child is not.

Mayer (1983) found that marital discord, poor sexual relationships between parents, and unwillingness of the perpetrator to seek sexual relationships outside the family characterize sexually-abusive families. Additionally, role reversals between parent and child were common (Mayer 1983). Marital discord may result from the power struggle between husband and wife. When perpetrators are men, their wives are usually oppressed (Herman, 1981). Because the perpetrator feels powerless outside the family or in the marital relationship, he/she will express sexual desires on family members who are considered less powerful. If the family is isolated, this task will be easier to accomplish. Reversing roles is an attempt to gain power, to have the child care for the perpetrator's emotional and physical needs.

Meiselman (1979) asserted that in sexually-abusive families, both the mother and father have been deprived of a normal family life. As a result, abusive parents are characterized as "inadequate socializing agents" (Oldershaw et al., 1986):

> ...[It] has been found that the mother's relationship with her own mother (the maternal grandmother) has been characterized by rejection and hostility. Fathers are described as hard working, respectable family men by neighbors but... his lack of experience with a good father figure deprived him of a realistic model for the role of patriarch that he desperately needed to play, and as a result he went too far in imposing authority in the form of incestuous sexual activity, on his children. (Meiselman, 1979, p. 92)

The social learning model proposed that abusive parents lack the skills to function properly in the home and society since they did not have appropriate models as children (Justice & Justice, 1976). The perpetrator may have had a parental role model that displayed the same desire for power and abused familial bases of power to satisfy those needs.

Although no single correlational factor is present in every abusive family, there are some commonalites: lack of strong communication between parents; mothers who are physically or psychologically absent; reversed roles; unequal power distribution between husband and wife; conflict resolved through scapegoating; nonsupport of family members; lack of autonomy among family members; confused communication and socially isolated members who are unable to cope with stress (Hasselt et al., 1988). Role reversals, isolation, scapegoating, and unequal marital relations all stem from a need for power which results in abuse.

Although it appears to be a sexual act, sexual abuse is motivated by urges to satisfy underlying emotional needs and a need to maintain control (Mayer, 1983). The occurrence of sexual abuse is exacerbated by our culture's gender socialization process and gender role expectations. The following sections will discuss family art therapy theory and research with sexually-abusive families.

FAMILY ART THERAPY THEORY

Wadeson (1980) felt that utilizing art therapy with families provides "a vehicle for the sharing of perceptions and the exposition of fantasy material" (p. 280). Through family art therapy, children can be heard and participate on an equal level with adults or older siblings. Wadeson found that even more submissive, withdrawn, and intimidated family members can find a voice through family art therapy.

According to Linesch (1993), family art therapy with sexual abuse survivors furnishes the following opportunities: self-expression, empowerment, improved communication and relationships. Linesch (1993) developed a family art therapy crisis intervention model that has the following treatment goals:

1. cognitive understanding of crisis dynamics
2. identification and expression of crisis-related affect
3. exploration of previous coping mechanisms and facilitation of adaptive coping through problem-solving
4. anticipatory planning
5. summary of gains made during the intervention process

Linesch (1993) found that comparing the perception of the family before and after a crisis provided access to underlying crisis dynamics. Crisis-related affect may be accessed through collage images or self-portraits. Problem solving lends itself well through collage work (Landgarten, 1993; Linesch, 1993). Anticipatory planning can focus on how the family can prevent future sexual abuse of their children.

An art therapy review is a reinforcing way to focus on familial gains. Linesch (1993) found that the crisis model was helpful for families in that it increased cognitive understanding and the expression of affect through art.

According to Riley (1994), family art therapy focuses on the following (p. 176):

1. the parent is the main focus of treatment in the early phase of therapy; however, the art work keeps the youth involved and allows him/her to make a statement in every session.

2. the attention is directed to the parent, and it is deflected away from the adolescent, which is syntonic with developmental needs and encourages the teenager to come to the session.

3. as the parent is led toward achieving or pretending to achieve adult skills, the child is relieved of inappropriate assignment of roles in the family.

4. the treatment of these families takes into consideration that a compromise will probably have to be made regarding the definitions of clear, hierarchical boundaries.

Riley (1994) stated that initial treatment issues should focus on the family's reluctance to expose their weaknesses and general mistrust of outsiders. "In this sense, the goal of family art therapy is not so much to change an individual in a family, but rather to help the client and family reinvent structure and transaction, resulting in new and more effective ways of interacting and communicating with each other" (Malchiodi, in Riley, 1994, p. 135). Since there is a loss of dignity when compelled to ask for help, Riley suggested nonstructured, information drawing exercises such as collages and group drawings initially. "Through collage, the members of the family can be described by their gender, affect, and behaviors, and the emotional temper of relationships can be demonstrated through adding color-coded connective lines" (Riley, 1994, p. 190). Intermediate treatment goals should facilitate communication and focus on family strengths. "Through art therapy the family is provided the opportunity to illustrate the family story and, aided by these illustrations, to discover a new, alternative ending to that legend" (Riley, 1994, p. 21). One exercise that was used was for a family to pick a fairytale, such as Red Riding Hood, and act out the story. Riley (1994) suggested art tasks that help the family review past coping skills and affirmative moments experienced during more functional periods. Secondary treatment goals should help the family regain socialization skills, new meaning for relationships, gender roles, and personal safety. Art tasks should assist the client in recognizing past family of origin patterns and how they relate to present family functioning. "The art tasks offers families a lens to observe themselves as though they were outside their system" (Riley, 1994, p. 35).

Kwiatkowska (1978), a forerunner in the field of family art therapy, designed an assessment that can be conducted during one session with a family. Her family art evaluation consisted of the following exercises (p. 86):

1. A free picture (one for which no subject is assigned; the patient and his family may draw whatever they wish).
2. A picture of your family.
3. An abstract family portrait.
4. A picture started with the help of a scribble.
5. A joint family scribble.
6. A free picture.

A session ranges to one to five hours depending on family size and ability to process material. The evaluation utilizes semihard, square-edged pastels. The counseling room is equipped with separate easels for each family member. An unusual aspect of this evaluation is the abstract family portrait. Kwiatkowska (1978) stated that these portraits "are usually the most time-consuming but also the most interesting of all the procedures; they bring up many highly-charged feelings and are the climactic point of the session" (p. 88). In addition to discussing the qualitative aspects of family artwork, Kwiatkowska (1978) provided a quantitative rating scale for the family art evaluation.

ART THERAPY WITH SEXUALLY-ABUSIVE FAMILIES

Very little information exists that utilizes art therapy with families that have experienced sexual abuse. A few studies use a group format when working with mothers of sexually-abused children. According to Shields (cited in Landgarten & Lubbers, 1991), treatment issues with sexually-abused mothers should focus on the following issues (p.112):

1. Inability to trust others because of past betrayals;

2. Impaired self-image marked by feelings of low self-esteem, limited knowledge of emotional states, and poor awareness of their own sexuality;

3. Denial of feelings and denial that the sexual abuse occurred;

4. Unreasonable expectations of appropriate roles and responsibilities of family members;

5. Failure to establish and enforce behavior and family limits;

6. Pent-up anger at their family of origin, their present family, and "the system";

7. Poor family communication;

8. Lack of assertiveness about meeting their own needs in the family;

9. Poor social skills and isolation;

10. Need for help with "practical" issues such as the social service and court systems, public assistance, household management, and parenting skills.

Shields used art therapy in a long-term, ongoing, support group for mothers of sexual abuse survivors. Varying in age, race, and economic background, 14 mothers participated in the study. Exploring emotional states, feelings, family issues, roles, boundaries, and communication were a few of the themes for the group. Family drawings were particularly revealing. "The placement of the abused child outside of the 'family line' at the bottom of the page seems representative of the typical family dynamic of scapegoating the victim" (Shields, in Landgarten & Lubbers, 1991, p. 124). Since many mothers were overwhelmed by the court and social services systems, Shields spent time discussing these feelings. Additionally, she focused on how mothers could protect their children from future abuse. Since many members were passive, quiet individuals, the art process allowed the opportunity to participate and communicate with others who shared a similar experience. The following study also focused on mothers of sexually-abused children.

Hagood (1991) worked with a group of 12 women on a weekly basis who had daughters who were sexually-abused. The purpose of the group was to help these women improve social skills, deal with feelings related to anger and betrayal, and improve their relationships with their daughters. Since mothers of sexual abuse survivors may unconsciously project hostility toward their own mothers onto their daughters (Brooks, 1983; Hagood, 1991), the My Mother/My Daughter exercise was used to illustrate this comparison. Yet, Hagood (1991) noticed that these drawings were marked by denial. Mothers typically rated their relationships with their daughters more positive than they actually were. The KFD, mandalas, triangulation, and "lost in a storm" were just a few of the exercises used. Overall, Hagood (1991) found that the group format improves social, parenting, and survival skills with this population.

Cross (cited in Linesch, 1993) utilized art therapy with mothers and children, who were sexually-abused . Mothers or care givers were worked in slowly to the art process. Through a twelve-week program, Cross hoped to build trust and self-respect, increase empowerment, and encourage expression of conflicts through art. Body image, secrets, monsters, guilt, and construction of a game were some of the group exercises. Cross found that all the children completing the secret drawing used black and red. According to Alschuler and Hattwick (1947), black has been associated with depressed affect whereas red has been associated with strong emotions, sometimes anger.

> There was a general attempt to control the anxiety stimulated during the creation of the pictures by encapsulating the images. Most of the children applied the colors in heavy, pressured strokes, sometimes allowing colors to bleed through the page. (Cross, in Linesch, 1993, p. 111-112)

Cross found the group provided the members with a sense of universality. Additionally, "they learned that they could use their power without resorting to force or manipulation, by clearly expressing their needs and setting boundaries" (in Linesch, 1993, p. 126). This study clearly illustrated the dynamics of working with mothers and their sexually-abused children.

Although these studies worked only with mothers of sexually-abused children, Malchiodi (1990) asserted that these didactic groups are beneficial for several reasons. First, the group provides understanding on how the mother and child interact. Second, the clinician may serve as a model through the art process. It is particularly powerful in teaching parenting skills. Last, the didactic encounter may improve the mother-child relationship. Both mother and child can participate on a similar level which facilitates communication (Rubin, 1984; Malchiodi, 1990).

SUMMARY

To date, art therapy with sexually-abusive families has focused primarily on mother-child relationships. Additional research is needed involving other family members such as siblings or other significant members of the household. For those families that plan to remain intact, incorporating the perpetrator in the family session may be an option. Many therapists consider it controversial to involve the perpetrator. This decision should consider the survivor, other family members, and the therapist's recommendations. The use of art therapy with a group of perpetrators may be helpful in defining appropriate boundaries, developing realistic expectations, and improving communication.

REFERENCES

Allport, G.W.: *The nature of prejudice.* Reading, MA, Addison-Wesley, 1979.
Alschuler, R.H., & Hattwick, L.B.: *Painting and personality.* Chicago, University of Chicago Press, 1947.
Astrachan, A. : *How men feel: Their response to women's demands for equality and power.* Garden City, NY, Anchor Press, 1986.
Breines, W., & Gordon, L.: The new scholarship on family violence. Signs: *Journal of Women in Culture and Society, 8(3)*: 490-531, 1983.
Brooks, B.: Preoedipal issues in a postincest daughter. *American Journal of Psychotherapy, XXXVII (1)*: 129-136, 1983.
Forward, S., & Buck, C.: *Toxic parents.* New York, Bantam Books, 1989.
Gomez-Schwartz, B., Horowitz, J. M., & Cardarelli, A. P.: *Child sexual abuse: Initial effects.* Newbury Park,CA, Sage, 1990.
Hagood, M.M.: Group art therapy with mothers of sexually-abused children. *The Arts in Psychotherapy, 18:* 17-27, 1991.
Hansen, J.C., Woody, J.D., & Woody, R.H.: *Sexual issues in family therapy.* Rockville, MD, Aspen Systems Corporation, 1983.
Hasselt, V.B., Morrison, R.L., Bellack, A.S., & Hersen, M.: *Handbook of family violence.* New York: Plenum Press, 1988.
Herman, J. L.: *Father-Daughter incest.* Cambridge, MA, Harvard University Press, 1981.
Justice, B. & Justice, R.: *The abusing family.* New York, Human Sciences Press, 1976.
Kwiatkowska, H.Y.: *Family therapy and evaluation through art.* Springfield, IL, Charles C Thomas, 1978.
Landgarten, H. B.: *Magazine Photo Collage.* New York, Brunner/Mazel, 1993.
Landgarten, H.B., & Lubbers, D.: *Adult art psychotherapy: Issues and applications.* New

York, Brunner/Mazel, 1991.

Linesch, D.: *Art therapy with families in crisis: Overcoming resistance through nonverbal expression.* New York, Brunner/Mazel, 1993.

Malchiodi, C.A.: *Breaking the silence: Art therapy with children from violent homes.* New York, Brunner/Mazel, 1990.

Mayer, A.: *Incest: A treatment manual for therapy with victims, spouses, and offenders.* Holmes Beach, FL, Learning Publications, Inc, 1983.

Meiselman, K. C.: *Incest.* San Francisco, Jossey-Bass, 1979.

Oldershaw, L., Walter, G.C., & Hall, D.K.: Control strategies and noncompliance in abusive mother-child dyads: An observational study. *Child Development, 57:* 722-732, 1986.

Riley, S: *Integrative approaches to family art therapy.* Chicago, Magnolia Street, 1994.

Rubin, J.A.: *Child art therapy: Understanding and helping children grow through art.* New York, Van Nostrand Reinhold, 1984.

Wadeson, H.: *Art psychotherapy.* New York, John Wiley & Sons, 1980.

Chapter 11

FAMILY ART THERAPY

P reviously, the case of Brian was discussed in Chapter 7. The following represents the session by session work with Brian and his mother. Since their social worker was conducting family therapy with Brian and his mother, Gabrielle, previously, she participated in the family art therapy. Refer back to Chapter 7 for the genogram and family history.

SESSION 1:

The cotherapist led the first session. She pulled the chairs away from the table since Brian often fidgets with the empty chairs. During the last family session, Brian tried to knock the table over. The purpose of this session was to introduce myself and prepare Brian and his mother for family art therapy. Gabrielle and Brian sat close to one another. The cotherapist asked how their weekend went. Gabrielle would often prompt Brian to tell what they did on the weekend. During the last part of the session, Brian created a painting using a spinning wheel. He could not stop adding paint, even when his mother and the cotherapist asked him to. Gabrielle related that it is often difficult for him to stop and he often tests boundaries. Brian clung to his mother, often to the point of hanging on her. At times, she seemed uncomfortable with his behavior. The cotherapist stressed that if he wants to touch his mother Brian can ask her for a hug, which he did.

SESSION 2:

Brian and his mother created separate, free drawings. Gabrielle began by drawing a bird house using colored pencil. The birdhouse was closed in with one small hole at the top. The bird's nest was highly protected in this house.

Figure 11-1. Mother's free drawing

This may reveal her desire to protect Brian. Other than the house, the drawing was empty and lifeless. She worked in a linear fashion suggesting a strong need for control. Brian drew a bird's nest perched precariously on the top of a high tree. The drawing became increasing violent with the rain and tornadoes. Again, images of circles and wedges appeared in his work. This drawing may depict Brian's perception that the environment is out of control and that his mother is not always there to protect him. While the mother was away getting food, two eggs fell to the ground. This may reflect Brian's resentment of his mother working. He drew the sun partially hidden by clouds and then blacked out the face of the sun. This may reveal Brian's strong feeling's toward his father who has not had contact with Brian for some time. His father is the one suspected of sexually abusing him.

Figure 11-2. Brian's free drawing

During the session, Brian hung on his mother. He was very resistant to the cotherapist 's and Gabrielle's directives. He felt uncomfortable with everyone watching him. The cotherapist offered a Nerf ball to Brian in order to help him feel more comfortable.

SESSION 3:

I suggested that Brian and his mother complete a joint, free drawing together. Gabrielle decided that they should make a city. Brian began by using black pastels to create a building. Gabrielle paralleled him by creating a tall building using soft colors and light strokes, a marked contrast to Brian's approach. This drawing differed from others in that Brian did not adopt a violent theme. In fact, he

tried to avoid violence. For instance, when he drew the large
television on top of the building, he said that it could crash to the
ground and break into pieces.

Figure 11-3. Joint free drawing

Next, he drew wires on the TV and anchored it to the surrounding
buildings so that it would not break. Brian drew himself leaving the
scene by riding on a rocket. His desire to escape was revealed in
previous drawings in individual therapy. Brian was very joyful about
his creation and even joked because his side of the paper was messy
and his mother's side was clean.

Gabrielle created two trees next to her building and Brian tried
to help. He began to get silly by making the tree into a man. When
the cotherapist asked what the man was saying, Brian said, "Fuck
you." He did not appear angry when he said this, but his mother
was shocked. Brian began to turn red because his mother was
admonishing him. The cotherapist stressed later that this was simply

an answer to her question. Brian was particularly violent towards his mother at the beginning of the session. He was not following directives and it became a power struggle. When he finally listened to his mother, he became angry and told her that she was making him angry. Brian did not appear to have the words to describe why he was angry and next he threw a jar lid at his mother and hit her in the face.

SESSION 4:

Brian opened the session by telling Gabrielle and me about his trip to the zoo. The cotherapist was unable to participate in this session. After talking for a few minutes, we began with the art activity, the scribble drawing. Although their eyes were closed, both Gabrielle and Brian moved their pencils in a very deliberate and controlled fashion. For instance, Gabrielle was making an image of a tree even though her eyes were closed. Using water color pencils, she shaded in the tree and put flowers by the roots. Like her birdhouse from the previous session, it was surrounded by a large amount of white space.

Figure 11-4. Mother's scribble drawing

Additionally, it paralleled the first drawing in that the image was on the left-hand side of the page. This is often associated with concerns with past experiences. Similarly, the pronounced roots may reveal issues with the past. Also, the circular treetop may suggest an uncertainty about her future direction. Brian created a series of symbols to represent an antismoking slogan. He worked mostly in black, possibly revealing depression.

Figure 11-5. Brian's scribble drawing

This drawing was regressed compared to his previous work. Circles and wedges also appeared in the drawing. He used heavy pressure, which may suggest anxiety.

Gabrielle was highly verbal during the session. She shared much about herself and appeared to bond well with this therapist. Gabrielle talked about the types of media that she liked to work in, her art major in college, and her recent decision to go back to school to earn her degree. Toward the end of the session, Brian had difficulty following directives.

SESSION 5:

The cotherapist led the session by reviewing the goals Brian had when he initially entered day treatment. His teacher and his mother were also present. When he first came into the program, Brian displayed aggressive behavior and had difficulty following directives. Although he still has problems when asked to complete a task, he has not demonstrated aggressive behavior. Another concern was that Brian continually used baby talk and hung on his mother. His teacher commented about how much improvement he had made, particularly when working with large groups of children. I noticed that his drawings were not as violent as they were in the beginning of art therapy. His confidence seems to have improved.

During the conversation, Brian said, "I am glad that they don't have sexual abuse in school." The cotherapist prompted him about this but Brian just said that he saw a commercial on TV and would not talk about it further. Brian has talked about sexual abuse with his mother's boyfriend. His first attempt to reveal the abuse was to a male psychologist. The cotherapist would like to have the mother's boyfriend participate in the sessions. His need to talk about the abuse seemed to be stronger.

SESSION 6:

I suggested that Brian and Gabrielle create a wish picture. In this drawing, they were to try and draw something that they wanted to change in their relationship. Gabrielle selected colored pencil and worked in a linear fashion. She drew Brian's room. Gabrielle said that the one thing that she would change about their relationship was having Brian clean up his room. She stated that he has a bad habit of leaving his toys laying around the house. She told Brian that it would make her happy if he made more of an effort to keep his room clean. As with her previous drawings, this drawing lacked people. Brian's drawing was more impoverished than his previous work. He tended to regress more during family therapy as compared to individual therapy. Brian drew his mother talking on the phone. He said that it made him angry that his mother was always talking on the phone. No matter where they went, she was always talking to someone. He drew his mother in red, a color associated with strong feelings and some-times anger (Alschuler & Hattwick, 1947). The stick figure drawing

Figure 11-6. Mother's wish picture

Figure 11-7. Brian's wish picture

may be a sign of resistance (Burns & Kaufman, 1972). He placed a barrier between himself and his mother, similar to his KFD. The remainder of his drawing was in black which may reveal depressive tendencies (Alschuler & Hattwick, 1947).

SESSION 7:

I suggested that Brian and Gabrielle create separate collages. They had a free choice of themes. Brian created a wish collage of all the things that he wanted such as CD players, stereos, TVs, VCRs, etc.

Figure 11-8. Brian's collage

Gabrielle's was in sharp contrast yet also represented a wish collage including gardens, outdoor scenes, fishing, etc.

Figure 11-9. Mother's collage

The materialistic bent of Brian's collage bothered Gabrielle. Brian's images were impulsively selected, cut, and pasted on the page, some of which extend beyond the border of the page. On the other hand, Gabrielle's images were carefully selected, cut, and pasted on the page.

Next, they created a collage together. Brian did not extend beyond the borders of the page for this collage. When Brian cut out pictures of guns, Gabrielle became upset and forbid him to paste any guns on the page. Brian did not listen and kept testing limits. He pasted the gun down and then was getting ready to glue the second gun on the page. Gabrielle agreed that he could put only one gun on the page, yet Brian began to glue the second gun down. Finally, he ripped the first gun off the page and continued on with the collage. Thereafter, they worked cooperatively and named the collage. Brian titled it the

Bruno Picture, after their dog. Brian's difficulty with boundaries was apparent during this session. First, his images on the individual collage extended off the page. Second, he tested his mother's limits with the use of guns on the collage.

Figure 11-10. Joint collage

SESSION 8:

In the last session, I did an art therapy review. During the session, I shared the clinical information related to their drawings. For instance, the first session drawings revealed Gabrielle's desire to provide a safe, protected environment for her son. On the other hand, Brian's perception of the environment was threatening and chaotic. The joint drawing of the city revealed boundary issues for Brian as well as his difficulty with limits. The regressed drawing style Brian used was related to his baby talk during the session. As you can see from Chapter 7, his drawing style during individual therapy was not as regressed. Brian did show some improvement during family work in that he attempted to deal with boundary issues and to reduce violent themes.

Brian was very aggressive towards his mother during the session. He admitted that he was deliberately trying to make her angry. The last part of the session was spent discussing anger issues. Brian related this to his father hitting his mother. He said that it was wrong, yet, he hits his mother often. This was the last art therapy session with the family. Brian and his mother continue to participate in family therapy with the cotherapist.

REFERENCES

Alschuler, R.H., & Hattwick, L.B.: *Painting and personality.* Chicago, University of Chicago Press, 1947.

Burns, R.C., & Kaufman, S.H.: *Actions, styles, and symbols in Kinetic Family Drawings (K-F-D): An interpretive manual.* New York, Brunner/Mazel, 1972.

Chapter 12

CONCLUSION

There are several assessments that are useful when working with sexual abuse survivors. The most widely researched instrument was the KFD, which reveals boundaries issues as well as the nature of relationships between family members. Encapsulation, role reversals, and isolation were common themes in the KFD's of sexual abuse survivors (Johnston, 1979; Goodwin, 1982; Cohen & Phelps, 1985; German, 1986; Kaufman & Wohl, 1992). When using the KFD with sexual abuse survivors, I have found that every member of the family seemed to be in a separate room. There was very little familial interaction. Human figure drawings and HTP's were particularly revealing when working with sexual abuse survivors.

Some writers have noted recurring images in the work of sexual abuse survivors. For instance, human figures drawn by survivors focus on the head and neglect the lower portion of the body (Malchiodi, 1990; Sadowski & Loesch, 1993). Additionally, several features, such as hands, feet, and pupils, were omitted. Spring (1988) found that eyes and wedges primarily characterize the work of this population. Phallic or vaginal trees and differential treatment of one window were found when using the HTP. Many of the graphic indicators cited in the literature were based on clinical observations. Only eyes and wedges were empirically examined. Another criticism is that the observations were made by individuals who were not art therapists or did not have training in art therapy. In order to provide validity and reliability for graphic indicators of sexual abuse, research needs to be conducted using children as well as adults representing both male and female survivors.

Research shows that art therapy may be helpful in working with memories of sexual abuse (van der Kolk, 1987; Burgess, 1988). This is particularly true if the client suffers from DID (Shapiro, 1988; Kluft,

1993; Jacobson, 1994). Some argue that art therapy gives rise to false memories of abuse (Ofshe & Watters, 1994). Also, there is a debate about whether art therapy represents actual memories. When creating art, my clients have discovered or triggered memories. Whether the art represented actual memories, I am not sure. I do know that it brought the person close to the truth about her past and helped abate the struggle with vague memories. This is essential in the healing process. In order to combat the criticisms in using art therapy with sexual abuse survivors, additional research is needed to explore the nature of working with traumatic memories through art.

Very little information exists on the use of drawings in court proceedings. Many writers agree that drawings can serve as evidence of abuse (Burgess et al., 1981; Kelley, 1984 & 1985; Landgarten, 1987; Miller et al. 1987; Boat & Everson, 1988; Lyons, 1993; Steward et al., 1993). There is controversy as to whether art therapists can qualify as expert witnesses. Although some have served as witnesses, they had to be backed up by a forensic psychologist or a psychiatrist in order to be considered credible. Additional information on legal issues and art therapy is needed. It would be helpful for those art therapists serving as expert witnesses or providing diagonistic evaluations to the court to write about their experiences and share their feelings about the legal process.

Combining art therapy with the case approach has yielded invaluable information regarding sexual abuse issues. Although not always effective for treating depression (Peacock 1991), most researchers found that art therapy helped the survivor's level of self-esteem, empowerment, and ability to problem solve (Stember, 1978; Kelley, 1984; Volgi-Phelps, 1985; Yates & Pawley, 1987; Dufrene, 1994; Brooke, 1995). In working with Brian, I found that art therapy was healing in that it gave voice to his anger regarding the abuse. Also, he began to deal with boundary issues which was a marked improvement compared to the beginning of therapy.

Group work with sexual abuse survivors has been very effective in raising levels of self-esteem and developing trust. One debate centers on the use of structured groups. Some researchers argue that the use of themes may be to emotive for some group members and inhibits the natural progress of the group (McNeilly, 1983, 1984; Waller, 1993). Also, theme-oriented groups may foster dependency on the therapist. On the other hand, some therapists feel that themes allow for bonding between members and provide focus. I found themes are helpful especially for those clients who have little experience with groups and creating art. For established groups, I feel that providing themes may foster dependency and limit the natural process of the group.

Another approach to treatment is family art therapy with survivors. According to the literature, these families are characterized by isolation, role reversals, secrecy, unclear boundaries, and unrealistic expectations (Justice & Justice, 1976; Hansen, 1983; Gomez, 1990). To date, most of the research on art therapy with sexually-abusive families has focused on mother groups or mother-child groups. This process was helpful for the mother to understand her child as a victim, not an instigator of the abuse. I found that family art therapy was particularly helpful in strengthening communication between the survivor and the nonperpetrating parent. Given that many survivors feel powerless and helpless, family art therapy provides an opportunity for the child to participate on an equal level with adults and express concerns regarding the abuse. Additional research is needed on using art therapy with a group of perpetrators. Art therapy may be helpful in establishing boundaries which are necessary for healthy familial relationships.

REFERENCES

Boat, B.W., & Everson, M.D.: Interviewing young children with anatomical dolls. *Child Welfare, LXVII(4):* 337-352, 1988.

Brooke, S.L.: Art therapy: An approach to working with sexual abuse survivors. *The Arts in Psychotherapy, 22(5)*: 447-466, 1995.

Burgess, E.J.: Sexually abused children and their drawings. *Archives of Psychiatric Nursing, 2(2)*: 65-73, 1988.

Burgess, A.W., McCausland, M.P., & Wolbert, W.A.: Children's drawings as indicators of sexual trauma. *Perspectives in Psychiatric Care, 19(2)*: 50-57, 1981.

Cohen, F.W. & Phelps, R.E.: Incest markers in children's art work. *Arts in Psychotherapy, 12*: 265-284, 1985.

Dufrene, P.: Art therapy and the sexually abused child. *Art Education, November:* 6-11, 1994.

German, D.: *The female adolescent incest victim: Personality, self-esteem, and family orientation.* Unpublished doctoral dissertation, Andrews University. Cited in Handler & Habenicht (1994), 1986

Goodwin, J.: Use of drawings in evaluating children who may be incest victims. *Children and Youth Services Review, 4*: 269-278, 1982 .

Gomez-Schwartz, B., Horowitz, J. M., & Cardarelli, A. P.: *Child sexual abuse: Initial effects.* Newbury Park, CA, Sage, 1990.

Hansen, J.C., Woody, J.D., & Woody, R.H.: *Sexual issues in family therapy.* Rockville, MD, Aspen Systems Corporation, 1983.

Jacobson, M.: Abreacting and assimilating traumatic, dissociated memories of MPD patients through art therapy. *Art Therapy: Journal of the American Art Therapy Association, 11(1)*: 48-52, 1994.

Johnston, M.S.K.: The sexually mistreated child: Diagnostic evaluation. *Child Abuse & Neglect, 3*: 943-951, 1979.

Justice, B., & Justice, R.: *The abusing family.* New York, Human Sciences Press, 1976.

Kaufman, B., & Wohl, A.: *Casualties of childhood: A developmental perspective on sexual abuse using projective drawings.* New York, Brunner/Mazel, 1992.

Kelley, S.J.: The use of art therapy with sexually abused children. *Journal of Psychosocial Nursing, 22(12)*: 12-18, 1984.

Kelley, S.J.: Drawings: Critical communications for sexually abused children. *Pediatric Nursing, 11*: 1985.

Kluft, E.S.: *Expressive and functional therapies in the treatment of multiple personality disorder.* Springfield, IL, Charles C Thomas, 1993.

Landgarten, H.: *Family art psychotherapy.* New York, Brunner/Mazel, 1987.

Lyons, S.J.: Art psychotherapy evaluations of children in custody disputes. *The Arts in Psychotherapy, 20:* 153-159, 1993.

Malchiodi, C.A.: *Breaking the silence: Art therapy with children from violent homes.* New York, Brunner/Mazel, 1990.

McNeilly, G.: Directive and non-directive approaches in art therapy. *The Arts in Psychotherapy, 10(4)*: 211-219, 1983. (Reprinted in *Incscape*, December, 1984).

Miller, T.W., Veltkamp, L.J., & Janson, D.: Projective measures in the clinical evaluation of sexually abused children. *Child Psychiatry and Human Development, 18(1)*: 47-57, 1987.

Ofshe, R., & Watters, E.: *Making monsters: False memories, psychotherapy, and sexual hysteria.* New York, Charles Scribner's Sons, 1994.

Peacock, M.E.: A person construct approach to art therapy in the treatment of post sexual abuse trauma. *The American Journal of Art Therapy, 29:* 100-109, 1991.

Sadowski, P.M., & Loesch, L.C.: Using children's drawings to detect potential child sexual abuse. *Elementary School Guidance & Counseling, 28:* 115-123, 1993.

Shapiro, J.: Moments with a multiple personality disorder patient. Pratt Institute *Creative Arts Therapy Review, 9:* 61-72, 1988.

Spring, D.: *Shattered Images: The phenomenological language of sexual trauma.* Chicago, Magnolia Press, 1993.

Stember, C.J.: Change in maladaptive growth of abused girl through art therapy. *Art Psychotherapy, 5(2)*: 99-109, 1978.

Steward, M.S.:, Bussey, K., Goodman, G.S., & Saywitz, K.J.: Implications of developmental research for interviewing children. *Child Abuse & Neglect, 17*: 25-37, 1993.

van der Kolk, B.A.: *Psychological Trauma.* Washington, DC, American Psychiatric Press, Inc., 1987.

Volgi-Phelps, V.: Letting the monsters out! *The Pointer, 29*: 35-40, 1985.

Waller, D.: *Group Interactive Art Therapy: Its Use in Training and Treatment.* New York, Routledge, 1993.

Yates, B.S., & Pawley, K.: Utilizing imagery and the unconscious to explore and resolve the trauma of sexual abuse. *Art Therapy, 7(1)*: 36-41, 1987.

Appendix I

INTERVIEW (5/15/96)

E: Ellen Horovitz, ATR - Director of Art Therapy Program at Nazareth College in Rochester, NY and Coordinator of Art Therapy at Hillside Children's Center in Rochester, NY

S: Stephanie Brooke - Interviewer

S: *When you are working with a sexual abuse survivor, what is involved in an art therapy assessment?*
E: Well, you know the kinds of assessments that I generally do. I follow a specific format, with adults or with children. I am not quite sure what you are asking.

S: *What types of assessments are you using to determine sexual abuse?*
E: The very first thing that I do is the Kinetic Family Drawing (KFD) because that gives me sociohistorical information about genograms and relationships. That usually gives me a point to start off from. The next thing that I do is the CATA, the Cognitive Art Therapy Assessment, just because it is free based-using drawing, painting, and clay. Using the CATA causes enough anxiety so that if somebody does have some issues that they are covering up and they may get a clue through that particular assessment. If there are issues that come up regarding spirituality and questions of forgiveness and sin, which often does come up with sexual abuse survivors, because they feel guilty and shamed and dirty and responsible, then I might conduct the BATA, the Belief Art Therapy Assessment. If I am looking for some cognitive and behavioral indices, I might do the Silver, for a comparison.

S: *What comes up on the Silver?*
E: Generally, in the Drawing From Imagination, you tend to see, a lot of... you know, she [Silver] talks about the projective emotional score, you tend to see a lot of negative themes that come up. Lots of snakes have come up, interesting enough, mixed with the bridal. She [Silver] has revised her text based on some of the information that I gave her last year. As a result, the test has been revised as well. She included some additional images, offering two pages as opposed to one page of images. With the greater variety you tend to get more sexual constructs that might come up. For instance, the whale has come up with some of the sexual abuse survivors that I have worked with at Hillside Children's Center. The whale has been paired with other images, often with a snake or knife, in a devouring format.

151

S: *From the research that I had done on my book, Tools of the Trade, it appeared that the Drawing From Imagination subsection was taken from Silver's Draw a Story Test.*
E: Yes, but that is more for adults. That is a depression scale. The Silver was created specifically for working with nonverbal clients, the deaf, who did not have the ability to form language skills, because they could do this assessment and respond much more readily than they could to a verbal task.

S: *Do you think that there are any other types of assessments that would be helpful?*
E: There are a lot of assessments that might be helpful. There are self-esteem inventories that might be helpful that are not even art therapy-oriented, such as Cooper's Self-Esteem Inventory or Beck's Depression Scale, that might give you more cognitive information compared to some of the indexes that we have available. The other thing that I think would be extremely helpful is the Diagnostic Drawing Series (DDS) that Barry Cohen developed because that would give you information on whether or not multiple personalities are at work. The DDS is pretty articulate in its ability to discern whether or not there is multiple personality going on. That assessment has been used not only by art therapists but by countless therapists nationwide.

S: *What do you think are some indicators of sexual abuse in art work?*
E: Some of the stuff that Dee Spring has talked about in her book has come up over and over again. You tend to see the paranoid eyes all over the place, the wedge shapes, red curtains in windows, and red chimneys. The indexes that Felice Cohen talked about back in the 80's when she printed her article on incest markers in children's artwork and Dee Spring's work comes up over and over again.

S: *Do you think that there are repressed memories of abuse? There is a big controversy in the literature regarding the validity of repressed memories and false memory syndrome. What are you thoughts?*
E: I reviewed the PBS tape that came out, *Divided Memories*, and I have mixed feelings about the whole subject. I certainly believe that some people can harbor repressed memories. I certainly believe that there are some therapists who can trigger memories that are untrue, for whatever their own reasons are to do that. There are some very unethical therapists. Yes, I think that there are people out there who can be very dangerous. On the other hand, I think that there are fewer of those people than there are good therapists, who are there not necessarily to assist the memories, a false crescendo, but in fact, to help people resolve some of those feelings that are coming up. So I think it can be both depending on who you are lucky or unlucky enough to be working with as a client.

S: *Do you think drawings represent actual memories?*
E: Yes, I absolutely feel that they are actual memories. They could be copied in a group situation. Certainly that could happen. It happens all the time. When you are talking about inner dialoguing that is going on and drawing from within, which

art therapy assists somebody to do, I don't think that is something that can be fabricated. Unless, in fact, you have a very disturbed patient that brings that kind of information to the therapist for whatever secondary gain he/she gets out of it. I have had client situations where that has occurred, where I have had very disturbed patients who would bring in stuff that they think that I would want to see. It takes awhile to cut through that. But it is rare.

S: *You have already been involved in a court proceeding that utilized art therapy assessments. What was that experience like for you?*
E: It was horrible [laugher]. It was really pretty awful. The reason it was so horrible was because it was out of my control. It was interstate, it was not within this state. Had it been in the state, I would have been able to travel and sit before the judge and talk about the assessments that I sent, and defend the artwork in person. I was not offered the opportunity. I was not given the opportunity. I was not asked to travel. If I had been asked by the State of Indiana to appear before the judge and travel, I would have done it of my own monies and my own volition. I was very very invested in the case, but they did not want me there. They just wanted the documentation of the work. And because I was not there to defend it, the judge ruled it out and dismissed the artwork. When you saw the pictures, they were so graphic... A man on top of this little girl, inserting his penis into her vagina. It does not get much more graphic than that. And that was my second session with the client.

S: *On what grounds did the judge dismiss the artwork?*
E: I don't know because I was not there. What I found out was that they had decided that the father, who was one of the perpetrators in a different way, he was neglectful and had exposed his children to the biological mother who you will remember was a hooker, who had tied up her kids and done it to them every which way, and inserted sticks in the little girl's vagina, the Sybil kind of stuff that you read about like tying up the kids and leaving them in the dark for a few days. He never stopped that type of abuse. Then he married a second woman who also was abusive to the kids, sexually. And her brother sexually abused the little girl at the age of six when she was in the care of the second wife. So while, he [father] was not a perpetrator himself, he was found guilty of neglect, leaving the kids naked out in the garage on mattresses and things like that. So, it was never proven, in fact, that he was a perpetrator. Based on his past relationships, I certainly would not have doubted it. They suggested that the father should take the kids back and they decided that therapy was no longer necessary for the children and yanked them out of the New York State foster home back to Indiana, to live with the father. I have never heard from them again. We were not allowed to follow up or to have contact.

S: *Do you think that an art therapist can be considered an expert witness?*
E: Absolutely. I mean, there are many people who would tear us to pieces, that would disagree with that. Dee Spring has her doctorate and can certainly defend her education and has written a book on Shattered Images that come up in the

work of the sexually abused. Yet, when she goes to court, she is torn to pieces as well. Lots of art therapists have gone to court and have been torn to pieces. I have not been given the opportunity to actually go, but my documentation, which was very solid and very grounded, and was in fact shown to an outside expert, a psychiatrist, agreed, concurred, and wrote a letter documenting his agreement with my findings, and they just ruled it out as immaterial, that it didn't matter, and that they didn't believe it. The children were sent back to the father. So unless you are right there in the chair, so-to-speak, to defend your documentation, you are not going to have much headway. And even if you are, it is still debatable if someone will consider an art therapist's testimony as expert. But as we are gaining stature from state to state and since board certification has happened, and licensing has really begun to happen nationwide, I think there will be less and less of that in the future. And art therapists will be called in for forensic situations to be expert witnesses. I think that it is beginning to tip in the other direction. I think it will happen, even with managed care, in the next ten years.

S: *So you think that drawings can serve as evidence of sexual abuse?*
E: I see the day, not very far off, that a person will digitally scan something across the INTERNET to me and ask me to do a forensic diagnosis based on information. I don't see that as far off at all. I am beginning to teach my students how to do that stuff. Technology is impacting every field. There are people on the WEB who are doing therapy on line.

S: *What kind of advice do you have for therapists using art therapy assessments with survivors or suspected survivors of sexual abuse?*
E: Be very careful how you word things, have additional supervision from a psychiatrist or a well-respected authority who would be less apt to be torn apart, to really know your information if you were to go to court because you will be torn apart. Having gone to court on different issues, I know it is important to have somebody sit down and proctor you, to do role modeling so that you know what to expect. It is very unnerving to be attacked and torn apart. I was attacked and torn apart as a social worker when I inherited a case at Hillside seven years ago. While I stood my ground and the case was ruled in my favor, it was a very unnerving experience. I spent about six hours with the lawyer for Hillside, being pummeled by the kinds of questions that I might expect. That prepared me for the attack on me and my field, so that I would not become defensive and angry.

S: *What kinds of questions did they ask you?*
E: What kind of validity could you possibly have with this drawing? How can you say that it was based on so and so? Who the hell is John Buck? Those kinds of things. And having to have the information at my fingertips to say the field has been around since 1963. What gives you the right to interpret it as a psychological interpretation? Well, I have taken PhD level clinical psychology courses at NYU that cover this information. I have taken the same courses that clinical psychologists have taken. In fact, I have studied this much more in depth. Research

indicates that psychologists don't give the chromatic versions while we do. So you have to have that kind of information there so that when a lawyer says that to you, you have the wherewithal to feed back, this is why I do this, this is how I do this, I am not just making this up as I go along. So I would say that preparation is the key element.

S: *It sounds like you have to know a lot about the history.*
E: Not so much the history of art therapy because they don't care about that. But more the history of psychological testing, which for you would be an easy thing to do since that is your area of expertise. So if you were to be an expert witness, I think you would fend very well as long as you could keep in check your feelings as they attack you. I say they, like they are sharks...

S: *It probably feels that way when they are questioning you.*
E: It does feel that way. It feels very demanding and unfair.

S: *That about covers it. Thank you for your time.*
E: You're welcome.

INTERVIEW 6/3/96

Dee Spring, Ph.D., A.T.R.-BC, BFCE, is a licensed psychotherapist in two states, a Board Certified Forensic Examiner, and the Executive Director of Earthwood Center in Ventura, California. Dr. Spring has specialized in the treatment of traumatic and dissociative disorders for 23 years. She was the first art therapist to use art therapy as an intervention tool with rape victims beginning in 1973. Later, she used this modality in the government-funded rape crisis center that she established in Placentia, California (1975-1981) as the first center to see victims face-to-face and use art therapy as the primary modality. Dr. Spring has presented at many professional conferences on art therapy, graphic indicators of sexual abuse, and traumatic and dissociative conditions. She designed, organized, and became the first instructor of the AATA Symposia program which focused on art therapy, sexual abuse, Dissociative Identity Disorder, and was awarded the American Art Therapy Association's Research Award for her research into graphic indicators. Her most recent book is *Shattered Images: Phenomenological Language of Sexual Abuse.* Her next book (in press) is titled, *Image and Mirage: Visual Language of Multiplicity.*

NOTE: Dr. Spring completed this questionnaire by mail. A majority of the questions were addressed in previous chapters of this book; therefore, the following represents those questions on which Dr. Spring provided additional information.

1. *Do you think that there are repressed memories of abuse? There is a big controversy in the literature regarding the validity of repressed memories and false memory syndrome. What are you thoughts?*

Traumatic memories are often repressed, or as in the case of Dissociative Identity Disorder, split off and retained by separate identities. There is no such thing as "false memory syndrome." This is a phrase coined by the False Memory Syndrome Foundation founded in 1992. Their research is based on normal memory because traumatic memory cannot be tested in a laboratory as this is unethical. Normal and traumatic memory are very different.

2. *Have you been involved in a court proceeding that utilized art therapy assessments. If so, what was that experience like for you?*

It is part of my job. As a trauma therapist for 23 years, it can be frustrating, highly charged, exciting, or depressing.

3. *Do you think that an art therapist can be considered an expert witness?*

Yes. I am an expert witness and Certified Forensic Examiner (BCFE) with the American Board of Forensic Examiners. Art therapists must have the proper credentials, A.T.R. - BC and be considered a specialist in particular areas to qualify.

They must be able to document their credentials and be accepted by the court to serve in this capacity. Years of experience are vital.

4. *Can drawings serve as evidence of sexual abuse?*

Yes. Use of my research serves as the base and falls under particular rules of evidence.

5. *What kind of advice do you have for therapists using art therapy assessments with survivors or suspected survivors of sexual abuse?*

Are the assessments documented? Is there a research base for the assessment? Do not jump to conclusions since all material in therapy is self-reporting, not hard evidence; symptoms, alone, are not enough.

INTERVIEW 6/10/96

F: Felice Cohen, formerly the Chief of Art Psychotherapy at the Texas Research Institute of Mental Sciences and the University of Texas, Mental Sciences Institute in Houston is a retired art therapist. She has had many years of experience working with sexual abuse survivors. Additionally, she published an article, "Incest Markers in Children's Artwork", along with her colleague, Dr. Randy Phelps (1985) in the Journal of Arts in Psychotherapy.

S: Stephanie Brooke - Interviewer

S: *When you are working with a sexual abuse survivor, what is involved in an art therapy assessment?*
F: Well actually, whether I was working with a sexual abuse survivor or any patient, I used the same assessment for all intakes I did. Remember that I worked primarily with children. However, I did do some family art therapy as well. So with the children, I always asked them to draw the House-Tree-Person, Draw a Person, and Draw a Picture of your Family. I gleaned a great deal of information from those drawings, whether the child was sexually-abused or not. However, with the sexually-abused child, there were some indicators that made me look twice at the drawing. For example, where the child placed herself in the family situation when she drew a family picture, how she saw herself when she drew a person, things of that sort. I would like to add here that I used Magic Markers, pencils, and 8" x 10" or 10" x 12" plain paper, so that the child could choose whatever media he/she wished. Of course, if she/he rejected the colors, this in and of itself is of value in the assessment. Further, I would like to say with regard to assessments to determine sexual abuse, I made every effort to involve the whole family in a family art therapy assessment. I used Hanna Kwiatowska's (1978) assessment which she used for family drawings that I applied as well to sexual abuse survivors. One thing that I think is important is that you have adult size easels for each member of the family. All easels should be the same height and in a semi circle with paper clipped to it and separate drawing material for each person in the family. The reason that all the easels are the same height even though we had a child in the room, was so that the child would not be tempted to go to the low easel. Where he or she goes is fine, then we lower the easel. This way we can determine who wants to stand next to whom, how the family interacts; a wealth of information is gleaned through this. As an example, I recall one particular session with a so called sexual abuse survivor, everyone in the family had drawn just the people in the family, those who were in the room. In the child's picture, there was another person, a man. In looking over the drawings, I mentioned in passing, that it was interesting that this child had drawn someone else in the family. Who is this person? I was informed that it was an uncle who visited there frequently. As it turned out, the uncle had been the perpetrator.

S: *What do you think are some indicators of sexual abuse in artwork?*
F: I have commented on this in my article, Incest Markers in Children's Artwork, published in *The Arts in Psychotherapy, 12*, p. 265-283. The article was inconclusive. I had hoped that other people would take up this research and carry it somewhere further. So far, I don't know of any research that continued on in this field. I was looking for indicators noted in Dr. Dee Spring's publication. Specifically, I was looking for eyes and wedges as sexual abuse indicators. Somehow, I can only say that there is nothing conclusive that indicates sexual abuse. You will also notice in my paper that one of my consultants was Lauretta Bender, M.D., who is the author of the Bender-Gestalt Test. I used many of her drawings that showed the same kind of indicators that I spoke of in the paper with Dr. Phelps.

S: *If someone suspects that they are a sexual abuse survivor, what therapeutic techniques would be helpful in his/her healing process?*
F: The first thing one must do is immediately try to remove the guilt feelings. Whether it be a child or an adult, there are always guilt feelings. The child always, almost without exception, has been told, if they told what happened that they would be in trouble, that mother would be killed or the dog would be killed, or a friend. There is a great deal of fear attached to this. In most of the writings on this subject, most authors feel that at some point the mother is aware of what is going on so that the child feels somewhat betrayed by the mother for not having stopped this behavior in the first place. So it is a very difficult thing to erase. As a matter of fact, one rarely erases all of these guilt feelings in the inner child. Most importantly, you must let the patient know that you accept him/her as a person who is not responsible for having had adults violate him/her in any way, shape, or form.

S: *Do you think that there are repressed memories of abuse? There is a big controversy in the literature regarding the validity of repressed memories and false memory syndrome. What are your thoughts?*
F: My thoughts would be that there definitely are repressed memories of abuse, whether they are false memories of abuse, or not. There are repressed memories of abuse from the survivor. I think a case in point was this adult woman who had been Miss America, from Atlanta, Georgia, who had repressed these things for many years. Not until she was an adult and married did this come to fruition; she revealed that she was sexually-abused by her father, a very prominent figure in the city. If my memory serves me correctly, there was someone in Florida who was in some high political position who also came forward after she was an adult who revealed that she too had been a survivor. Memories did not come to the fore for them until something triggered them. Evidently, in many cases, these memories are not triggered until the person is much older. I do believe that there may be false memory syndromes. In cases of divorce, where one parent would say that your father did this to you, someone did this to you, then the child picks this up. Again, it is not the child's fault because they were only trying to please the adult in the family. It would be very difficult to tell if the memories of sexual abuse were real or false; however, in many of the cases that I saw, the child had been

examined by a physician and it was determined that there had been penetration, vaginal warts, or any other evidence that made us realize that, medically, this child had been sexually-abused.

S: *Do you think drawings represent actual memories?*
F: I don't know who amongst us does not have repressed memories, whether about abuse or anything else regarding childhood experiences. There is no doubt in my mind that art therapy assessments are helpful when working with memories of abuse, whether they be vague or not. I think that they do represent actual memories. And I do think that art therapy is helpful when working with vague memories of abuse.

S: *Have you been involved in a court proceeding that utilized art therapy assessments? What was that experience like for you?*
F: It was horrible for me. Interestingly enough, two days ago, I attended a symposium at the University of Houston. One of the subjects discussed was this very same issue as to who is considered an expert witness. An art therapist cannot be considered an expert witness. The only persons that can be considered an expert witness are a forensic psychologist or a psychiatrist. I am enclosing for you, Daubert's Questions for Expert Witnesses (see Appendix II), since this is what lawyers use. When I was in court, I was asked if I actually saw the incident take place. "Children draw all kinds of things, this is in quotes, what makes you an expert? Everybody's child has drawn figures that are not necessarily attractive." In my paper, children drew unusual renditions of chimneys, trees, this does not make them sexually-abused children. Every experience that I have had in court, and I have had many of them, were degrading. I was made to feel that my profession was of no value. I certainly did not have the credentials that Daubert requested for expert witness. Even a PhD without certain defined necessities in this questionnaire cannot be expected to be an expert witnesses.

S: *Do you think that drawings can serve as evidence of sexual abuse?*
F: It depends on where you want to show this evidence of sexual abuse. You have to remember that we have nothing to show what children draw whether sexually-abused, physically abused, or emotionally abused is definitive. We have nothing yet. It is too early for us to consider this, in my judgment. I think much more scientific research needs to be done before we can answer that.

S: *What kind of advice do you have for therapists using art therapy assessments with survivors or suspected survivors of sexual abuse?*
F: Carry on. Do exactly what you are doing and also try and see if you can have a medical backup. Get a doctor to examine the child to see whether or not any of the indicators that I mentioned earlier have some validity. I think we have a great opportunity in having the child or the survivor express themselves in a nonthreatening way through art therapy. In closing, let me say that we do not have to be expert witnesses. I certainly would not want anybody to have to go through

what I went through on the witness stand for 15 or 20 cases in my professional life. It isn't worth it and nothing is accomplished. For some reason, it seems to me, that the perpetrator always seems to have the finest attorney while the child is represented by the county. And the county has people working for them in the district attorney's office who are right out of law school, who have little knowledge, and who only rotate through a case. In other words, I can recall one case in particular where there were four different attorneys ascribed to one case. The child is at a disadvantage to begin with. You can't do much about that. If you are looking for help from the district attorney's office and these nacient lawyers, you're in trouble. I hope that this may have been some help to you.

S: *Yes it has. It has been very informative and interesting. Thank you, Felice.*

Appendix II

DAUBERT'S
QUESTIONS FOR EXPERT WITNESSES

EXPERT QUALIFICATIONS:
- name
- address
- occupation
- present employment
- past employment
- educational background
- current professional involvement
- membership in professional societies
- field of expertise
- purpose and nature of consultation
- research
- what scientific testing did you undertake
- findings and opinions
- definitions

PROPOSED TESTIMONY IS SUFFICIENTLY TIED TO FACTS OF CASE SO THAT IT WILL AID THE FINDER OF FACT IN RESOLVING A FACTUAL DISPUTE:
- what does your testimony concern?
- in your opinion, how does that testimony relate to the nature of this suit (or its underlying issues)?
- do you believe the research you have done could have been done by the average lay-person (that is without your type of education or experience)?
- do you consider the research you have done to be decipherable by the average lay-person?
- do you feel your testimony will better aid the finder of fact to understanding the work you will present?

TESTING OF THE THEORY OR TECHNIQUE (FALSIFIABIL-
ITY):
- what theory/technique did you use in your research?
- how often do you use this theory/technique?
- do you use this theory/technique in other subject areas, or is it unique to the subject matter addressed in this case?
- how did you test this theory/technique?
- how many times did you test your theory/technique?
- when did you test your theory/technique?
- did you use the same testing method every time to test for accuracy
- did anyone, other than yourself, test your theory/technique for accuracy?
- what test did that person use?
- when did that person do his/her testing?
- what were the results?

EXTENT TO WHICH THE TECHNIQUE RELIES UPON
SUBJECTIVE INTERPRETATION OF THE EXPERT:
- does the technique you used generally require subjective or objective interpretation among others in your field?
- was the technique used in your research interpreted subjectively or objectively?
- do you feel another person in your field would have interpreted your technique the same as you have?
- is there a way to cross-check the subjective interpretation for accuracy?
- did such cross-checking take place?
- what were the results?

WHETHER THE THEORY/TECHNIQUE HAS BEEN
SUBJECTED TO PEER REVIEW OR PUBLICATION:
- has your theory/technique been published?
- where was it published?
- when was it published?
- where there any criticisms?
- what was the nature of the criticisms?
- has your theory/technique been reviewed by your peers?
- by whom was it reviewed by?
- when was it reviewed?
- what was their opinion of your technique after having reviewed it?

THE THEORY/TECHNIQUE'S KNOWN OR POTENTIAL RATE OF ERROR:

- does your theory/technique have a known or potential rate of error?
- what is that rate of error?
- how did you arrive at that rate of error?
- is that rate of error common for the theory/technique you used?
- did you carefully consider alternative causes or theories?
- what makes yours the best to use or most reliable?

GENERAL ACCEPTANCE OF THE THEORY/TECHNIQUE BY THE RELEVANT SCIENTIFIC COMMUNITY:

- is the theory/technique you used generally accepted by the scientific community within which you belong?
- by what means is it generally accepted and relied upon?
- by what groups/organizations is it generally accepted and relied upon?
- how long has it been generally accepted?

NON-JUDICIAL USES WHICH HAVE BEEN MADE OF THE THEORY/TECHNIQUE:

- have you used this theory/technique outside the purposes of litigation?
- in what instances?
- when?
- where?
- was the theory/technique used, consistent from those instances until now?
- was the theory/technique altered this time because of the litigation?

AUTHOR INDEX

A

Alexander, P.C., 94, 101
Allport, G.W., 123,131
Alschuler, R.H., 11, 14, 130, 131, 139, 141, 144
Alpert, J., 44,54
American Phsychological Assoc., 42, 45, 51
Anderson, F.E., 95, 96, 101
Astrachan, A., 124, 131

B

Barakat, L.P., 18, 26
Barbieri, M.K., 56, 60
Bardos, A.N., 26
Bass, E., 47, 51
Battle, J., 95, 101
Bays, J., 61
Becker, J., 61
Bellack, A.S., 131
Bender, L., 159
Benedek, E.P., 57, 59, 60, 61
Bepko, C., 114, 121
Berliner, L., 56, 57, 58, 60, 61
Betensky, M., 10, 11, 14
Beutler, L.E., 39, 102
Blitz, R., 54
Bloom, S.L, 46, 51
Blume, E.S., 41, 51, 109, 111, 113, 114
Boat, B.W., 58, 60, 146, 147
Bowers, J., 42, 48, 51
Braun, B.G., 48, 51
Breines, W., 124, 131
Brenneis, C.B., 40, 41, 44, 47, 51
Briere, J., 41, 42, ,43, 51
Briggs, F., 28, 29, 36, 68, 73, 74
Brittion, W.L., 8, 14, 35, 38, 82, 85
Brooke, S.L., vi, 17, 24, 25, 33, 36, 78, 86, 93, 94, 95, 96, 100, 101, 111
Brooks, B., 130, 131
Buck, C., 123
Buck, J.N., 20, 21, 25, 68, 74, 131
Burgess, A.W., 58, 60, 66, 74

Burgess, E.J., 27, 30, 31, 34, 36, 48, 51, 145, 146, 147
Burns, R.C., 19, 20, 21, 25, 32, 36, 111, 113, 116, 121, 141, 144
Burr, W., 54
Bussey, K., 62, 148
Bybee, E., 35, 36

C

Cabacunagan, L.F., 19, 25
Cardelli, A.P, 74, 131, 148
Carozza, P.M., 27, 28, 34, 36, 98, 99, 101
Case, C., 33, 35, 36, 65, 70, 74
Ceci, S.J., 43, 51
Chantler, L., 27, 28, 29, 36
Chase, D.A., 30, 31, 35, 36
Chernin, K., 109, 121
Chu, J.A., 42, 51
Clark, H., 74
Cohen, B.M., 22, 25
Cohen, F.W., 31, 32, 34, 35, 36, 48, 51, 59, 60, 104, 110, 122, 145, 147, 152, 158-161
Cohen-Liebman, M.S., 29, 34, 37, 57, 58, 59, 60
Conte, J., 41, 43, 52, 58
Conte, J.R., 57
Corder, B.F., 96, 101
Corkery, J.M., 52, 74
Corsini, R.J., 7, 8, 14
Corwin, D.L., 61
Coulson, K.W., 65, 74
Coutois, C., 43, 52, 58, 60
Crago, M., 39, 102
Cummings, J.A., 19, 25

D

Dachinger, P., 5, 15
Dalley, T., 33, 35, 36, 65, 66, 70, 74
Davies, J.M., 52
Davis, L., 42, 43, 47, 48, 51, 111, 122
Dawes, R.M., 46, 52

167

SUBJECT INDEX

A

American Academy of Child & Adolescent Psychiatry, 57–58
American Art Therapy Association, 4, 156
American Professional Society on the Abuse of Children, 57–58
Anger, 10, 63, 64, 65, 66, 67, 69, 70, 71, 86, 95, 96, 98, 100, 105, 106, 107, 110, 114, 116, 129, 130, 137, 139, 146
Anxiety, 28, 70, 71, 72, 79, 80
Archetypes, 7, 70, 71
Art expression, v,3–4, 6–12
Art media, 9–12
Art therapy, 5–6, 45, 48–51, 65–73
Art therapy assessments, 17–25, 58–60, 157, 158–159

B

Beck's Depression Inventory, 72, 152
Belief Art Therapy Assessment, 151

C

Case work with survivors, 65–73, 76–89
Circles, 32, 34, 71, 73, 89, 105, 106, 118, 134, 138
Clowns, 30
Cognitive Art Therapy, 8–9
Collages, 69, 107, 114, 126, 127, 141–143
Color, 11–12, 21, 22, 34–35, 70, 73, 83, 84, 85, 104, 105, 130
Cooper Self-Esteem Inventory, 152
Culture Free Self-Esteem Inventory, 95
Curative Climate Instrument, 98

D

Denial, 28, 43, 58, 71, 107, 129, 130
Depression, 24, 30, 34, 64, 68, 70, 72, 73, 85, 109, 116, 118, 130, 138, 146, 152
Development Art Therapy, 8
Diagnostic Drawing Series, 22, 152

(continued)

Dissociation, 34, 42, 43, 64, 118
Dissociative Identity Disorder, vi, 49, 50, 51, 66, 145, 156
Draw a Person, 18, 59, 99, 158
Dreams, 7, 8, 111,–114

E

Eating disorders, 70, 98, 109, 121
Encapsulation, 31, 33, 34, 69, 73
Evaluations of sex abuse, 57–58, 153
Expert testimony, 55–57, 59–60, 153–154, 157, 160, 163–165
Eyes, vi, 29, 30, 70, 97, 107, 114, 118, 145

F

False Memory Syndrome, 46–47, 50, 156
Family art therapy, 126–131, 133–144
Family Centered Circle Drawings 20
Family Drawings, 30–32, 109–111, 158
Floating images 34, 68, 70
Forgetting 41–44

G

Genogram, 77
Gestalt Art Therapy, 7–8
Graphic Indicators of Abuse, 27–36, 151–152, 159
Group Therapy, 9, 91–101, 97, 103–121
Guilt, 12, 29, 64, 66, 71, 98, 114, 130, 159

H

Hearts, 33, 67, 70, 71, 104, 121
House drawings, 32
House-Tree-Person Test, 20–21, 59, 145
Human Figure Drawing Test, 17–18
Human Figure Drawings, 27–30
Hypnosis, 45, 71

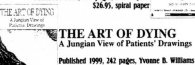

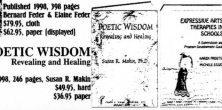

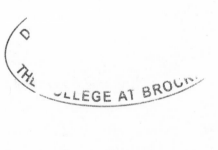